Human Health and Disease

Richard Fosbery

Series editor
Fred Webber

CAMBRIDGE
UNIVERSITY PRESS

PUBLISHED BY THE PRESS SYNDICATE OF THE UNIVERSITY OF CAMBRIDGE
The Pitt Building, Trumpington Street, Cambridge CB2 1RP,
United Kingdom

CAMBRIDGE UNIVERSITY PRESS
The Edinburgh Building, Cambridge CB2 2RU, United Kingdom
40 West 20th Street, New York, NY 10011-4211, USA
10 Stamford Road, Oakleigh, Melbourne 3166, Australia

First published 1997

Printed in the United Kingdom at the University Press, Cambridge

Typeset in Sabon 11/14 pt

Designed and produced by Gecko Ltd, Bicester, Oxon

A catalogue record for this book is available from the British Library

ISBN 0 521 42159 4 paperback

This book is one of a series produced to support individual
modules within the Cambridge Modular Sciences scheme.
Teachers should note that written examinations will be set
on the content of each module as defined in the syllabus.
This book is the author's interpretation of the module.

Front cover photograph: Barry Dowsett/Science Photo Library

Contents

Acknowledgements

The author wishes to express his thanks to Dr Roland Salmon of the Public Health Laboratory Service for his valuable comments on the manuscript.

Photographs

2.3, CE Gilbert/ICEH; 2.4, 3.4, Biophoto Associates/SPL; 2.5, Oxfam; 2.6, UNICEF/Bert Demmers; 2.7, Hulton Deutsch Collection; 2.8, 2.9, 4.5, 7.2, Syndication International; 3.2, 4.2, 5.1, 6.24, CNRI/SPL; 3.3, 3.14, Audio Visual Services (Loughborough University); Alfred Pasieka/SPL; 4.3, Tony Brain/SPL; 4.8, Publiphoto Diffusion/SPL; 5.2, HJ Davies/WHO; 5.4, Omikron/SPL; 5.6, NIBSC/SPL; 5.7 Kari Lounathaa/SPL; 5.8, T Falise/WHO; 6.3, 6.8, 6.11, Biophoto Associates; 6.13, JC Revy/SPL; 6.19, Bernard Pierre Wolf/SPL; 6.20, Associated Press; 7.3, Tony Stone Images/ Andrew Errington; 7.5, Astrid & Hans-Frieder Michler/SPL; 7.6, Paramount Pictures/Kobal Collection.

Diagrams

1.1, adapted from *Understanding Cancer and its Treatment*, ABPI; 2.1, from *Dietary Reference Values, A Guide* Department of Health, 1991, HMSO; 3.6, adapted from *Advanced Biology Principles and Applications, Study Guide* CJ Clegg *et al*, 1996, John Murray; 3.8, 3.10, 3.15, adapted from *Essentials of Exercise Physiology* McArdle *et al*, 1994, Lea and Febiger; 3.11, adapted from *Textbook of Physiology and Biochemistry* Bell *et al*, 1976, 9th ed. Churchill Livingstone; 3.12, adapted from *Enzymes, Energy and Metabolism* Ingle *et al*, 1986, Studies in Advanced Biology No.3, Blackwell; 3.13, *Physiology of Fitness* Sharkey, 1990, 3rd ed. Human Kinetics Books; 4.1, adapted from Tetley, *Biological Sciences Review*, May 1990; 4.4, adapted from *Smoking* ASH, 1994; 4.6, from *Coronary Heart Disease Statistics* Boaz & Rayner, 1995, British Heart Foundation; 5.5, adapted from Brown, *Inside Science, New Scientist*, 18 April 1992; 5.9, from the Global TB programme of the World Health Organisation; 5.10, 6.15, adapted from *Biology of Microorganisms* Brook *et al*, 1994, Prentice-Hall; 6.1, adapted from *Immunology* Roitt *et al*, 1989, 2nd ed. Churchill Livingstone; 6.7, 6.16, 6.18, adapted from *Medical Immunology for Students* Playfair & Lydyard, 1995, Churchill Livingstone; 6.21, from the World Health Organisation internet site; 7.1, adapted from *Drugs and the Brain* Snyder, 1986, Scientific American Library, WH Freeman & Co.

Tables

2.3, 2.4, 2.5, 2.6, data from *Dietary Reference Values for Food Energy and Nutrients for the United Kingdom*, 1991, HMSO; 2.7, data from *The Food Labelling Regulations 1996*, Statutory Instruments 1996 No.1499, HMSO; 2.8, *Energy and Protein Requirements*, Report of a joint FAO/WHO/UNU meeting, 1995, World Health Organisation; 2.10. adapted from *Diet and Nutrition Card, Student Activity Sheet*, 1994, World Vision UK; 3.1, 3.2, data from *Human Physiology, Foundations and Frontiers* Schauf *et al*, 1990, Times Mirror/Mosby College Publishing; 4.1, data from ASH Factsheet No.4; 4.2, data from ASH Factsheet No.1, and *Coronary Heart Disease Statistics* Boaz & Rayner, 1995, British Heart Foundation; 4.4, 4.5, World Health Organisation MONICA Project, 1989; 5.2, 5.3, 5.4, from the World Health Organisation internet site; 5.5, data from *Biology of Microorganisms* Brook *et al*, 1994, Prentice-Hall; 7.4, data from Alcohol Concern Factsheets No.9, 21 and 25.

Health and disease

What is health?

Health is difficult to define satisfactorily. It is often defined as a person's physical, mental and social condition. Health may be good or poor. Good health is more than just being free from disease. It is often linked to happiness and a fulfilling life. Someone who is healthy feels good physically and has a positive outlook on life, is well adjusted in society and is able to undertake the physical and mental tasks they meet in everyday life without too much difficulty.

Everyone is born with a genetic potential for growth and development. People need good health to grow and realise their potential and to play a full and active part in society. They can only do this if they live in an environment free from serious hazards to health. The World Health Organisation (an agency of the United Nations) maintains that good health is a fundamental human right and in its programme *Health for All by 2000* hopes to reduce the serious threats from disease that overshadow human existence. To enjoy good health, a person needs proper shelter, nutrition, exercise, sleep and rest. Good hygiene reduces the chances of infection. Access to medical and dental care ensures that health can be monitored and illnesses treated.

What is disease?

Just as health is difficult to define, so is **disease**. Put simply, a disease (or illness) is a disorder or malfunction of the body which leads to a departure from good health. It is usually a disorder of a specific tissue or organ due to a single cause. However, some diseases, such as heart disease, may have many causes and are described as **multifactorial**.

Diseases are characterised by signs and symptoms that are physical, mental or both. People who are ill may report their symptoms to a doctor. Symptoms give an indication of the nature of the disease. By examining and questioning their patients and carrying out tests, doctors identify signs of disease and make a diagnosis. Some diseases are **acute**, having a sudden onset with rapid changes. For example, the symptoms of influenza appear very quickly, within a few days of being infected. Acute diseases last for a short time. The effects of long-term, or **chronic**, diseases continue for months or years. Many chronic diseases are extremely debilitating.

Apparently healthy people may not obviously be afflicted with any disease, but their living conditions, diet or personal behaviour may be putting them at risk of developing chronic diseases which only manifest themselves in later life. You will read more about this in chapter 4.

Categories of disease

There are different ways of classifying disease. For example, it is possible to distinguish between physical and mental diseases, or between infectious and non-infectious ones. Nine broad categories are recognised (*table 1.1*), although some diseases are classified into more than one category. For example, some mental diseases are caused by physical changes that occur in the brain. This means that they can be classified as both physical and mental diseases.

Category of disease	Cause of disease	Examples
physical	permanent or temporary damage to any part of the body	leprosy, multiple sclerosis
infectious	organisms which invade the body	measles, malaria
non-infectious	any cause other than invasion by an organism	stroke, sickle cell disease
deficiency	poor diet	scurvy, night blindness
inherited	an inherited genetic fault	cystic fibrosis, haemophilia
degenerative	gradual decline in body functions	coronary heart disease, Huntington's disease
mental	changes to the mind, which may or may not have a physical cause	schizophrenia, claustrophobia
social	social behaviour, such as drug misuse	drug dependence, e.g. dependence on alcohol
self-inflicted	wilful damage to the body by a person's own actions or behaviour	attempted suicide, lung cancer

● *Table 1.1* Different categories of disease

Physical diseases

Physical diseases are associated with permanent or temporary damage to part of the body. This category includes *all* the other categories, except the less severe mental diseases where there is no sign of any physical damage to the brain.

Infectious diseases

Organisms which live in or on our bodies and gain their nutrition from us are called **parasites**. If they cause disease they are known as **pathogens**. **Infectious diseases** are those caused by pathogens such as viruses, bacteria, fungi, protoctists, worms and insects (e.g. lice). They are also called 'communicable diseases', because the pathogens are transmitted from person to person or from animal to person. Some infectious diseases, such as the common cold, measles, chickenpox and athlete's foot, may be transmitted during normal social contact. Others are transmitted in special ways such as through water, food or sexual contact. People can be infected with a pathogen, but not have any symptoms of disease. These people can transmit the disease, but because they are not ill they are often difficult to identify. They are described as **carriers** of infectious disease. *Table 1.2* lists some of the ways in which infectious diseases are transmitted.

Non-infectious diseases

All the diseases that are *not* caused by pathogens are termed **non-infectious diseases**. Therefore this category includes all the categories that follow.

Some diseases have one cause, for example inherited diseases and dietary deficiency diseases. Other diseases are more complex and are caused by many factors. Examples of multifactorial diseases are cancers and heart disease, which are often caused by interactions between genetic and environmental factors, such as diet.

Deficiency diseases

Deficiency diseases are nutritional diseases caused by an inadequate diet. If the diet does not supply sufficient energy for months or years, then people starve. Although most of the world's population have enough to eat, many children suffer from malnutrition because they do not have enough energy-containing foods in their diet. Also they do not receive enough essential nutrients such as proteins, vitamins and minerals and, as a consequence, suffer from several deficiency diseases, such as iron-deficiency anaemia, scurvy (deficiency of vitamin C), night blindness (vitamin A), and rickets (vitamin D). These diseases also occur in people who have enough to eat, but do not eat a balanced diet as one or more of the essential nutrients is missing or in short supply.

Method of transmission	Comments	Examples	Type of causative organism
airborne	droplets in the air or on dust	influenza	virus
		TB	bacterium
		chickenpox	virus
		pneumonia	fungus or bacterium
water-borne	water is contaminated by human faeces	cholera	bacterium
		typhoid	bacterium
		schistosomiasis	worm
		hookworm	worm
		dysentery	protoctist or bacterium
food-borne	food is contaminated by human faeces or by human carriers, or by flies or rodents	food poisoning	virus or bacterium
		typhoid	bacterium
		cholera	bacterium
insect-borne	insect vectors carry pathogens	malaria	protoctist
		sleeping sickness	protoctist
		yellow fever	virus
sexually transmitted	pathogens transmitted from infected host during sexual intercourse	AIDS/HIV	virus
		herpes	virus
		genital warts	virus
		non-specific urethritis	bacterium
		gonorrhoea	bacterium
		vaginal thrush	fungus
direct contact (contagious diseases)	spread by skin contact or in saliva	chickenpox	virus
		tinea (athlete's foot and ringworm)	fungus
		oral thrush	fungus
		herpes	virus
		polio	virus

● **Table 1.2** Methods of transmission of some infectious diseases. Some diseases have more than one method of transmission including some not shown here, for example HIV infection can pass from mother to child across the placenta

Inherited diseases

In Britain, cystic fibrosis is the most common inherited or genetic disease; it is rarely found in non-Caucasian populations. Sickle cell disease is most common in tropical Africa. These two genetic diseases (or genetic disorders as they are often called) are present from birth. They are extremely debilitating diseases which severely restrict the life of people who inherit them. Both can be treated, but both are incurable. *Table 1.3* lists the main types of genetic disease and their patterns of inheritance.

Genes mutate. The sequence of bases in DNA can change because of a substitution, a deletion or an insertion. In most cases these mutations produce alleles that are recessive to the normal allele. People who have cystic fibrosis have inherited a mutant allele from each of their parents. The parents do not have the disease as their normal allele is functioning correctly. They are described as **genetic carriers**. Some mutations, however, give rise to dominant alleles. This is the case with Huntington's disease, which can be inherited from one parent only.

Many inherited diseases such as sickle cell disease, phenylketonuria and haemophilia (see *Central Concepts in Biology* in this series) develop from birth. Others, such as Huntington's disease (see *Applications of Genetics* in this series) do not become apparent until much later, sometimes after a person has had children.

Type of genetic disease	Pattern of inheritance

Mutation of one gene
 autosomal:
   recessive allele (e.g. cystic fibrosis)
   dominant allele (e.g. Huntington's disease)
 sex linked:
   (e.g. haemophilia, muscular dystrophy)
	monohybrid inheritance; relatives are at risk of inheriting the same allele

Chromosome mutation change in number of chromosomes (e.g. Down's syndrome)	no pattern; relatives are at a low risk of inheriting the same disorder
change in structure of chromosomes (e.g. fragile X syndrome)	inherited in the same way as monohybrid inheritance
Multifactorial (e.g. most cancers, heart disease)	no pattern; environmental factors also contribute to development of the disease

● **Table 1.3** Types of genetic disease

SAQ 1.1

Explain, with the use of a genetic diagram, how two people who do not have phenylketonuria can have a child with this inherited disease.

Some genetic disorders are caused by chromosome mutations, rather than by individual gene mutations. There are two types:

■ changes in chromosome number;
■ changes in chromosome structure.

Changes in chromosome number usually occur during meiosis when chromosomes fail to separate properly. As a result cells contain either too many, or too few, chromosomes. This causes an imbalance in genetic material which disrupts physical and mental development. For example, some people with Down's syndrome have 47 chromosomes rather than the normal 46, with an extra copy of chromosome 21. Fragile X syndrome is an example of a change in chromosome structure. Like Down's syndrome, it is a form of retarded mental development. Part of the X chromosome is very narrow and often breaks when prepared for viewing under the microscope (hence the name fragile X). The cause is a large number of repeated base sequences and this mutation is inherited in the same way as a recessive mutation such as haemophilia. Just as with haemophilia, fragile X syndrome is more common amongst boys.

SAQ 1.2

Draw a genetic diagram to show how a boy can inherit fragile X syndrome from his mother who is a carrier of the condition.

Degenerative diseases

As we age, parts of the body work less efficiently. This may happen because the body's repair mechanisms begin to fail. These failings are associated with characteristics of ageing such as short-term memory loss, poor circulation and reduced mobility. However, degenerative diseases are not necessarily associated with growing old. Even in youth or middle age, a gradual loss of function in one or several organs or tissues can occur, associated with a progressive destruction of specialised cells. Sometimes this can happen because the defence system (the immune system – see chapter 6) begins to attack the body's own cells. As degenerative diseases progress, specialised cells are replaced by scar tissue. Deficiencies of nutrients during childhood may be the cause of a degenerative disease later in life, through restricting the full development of tissues.

There are three major types of degenerative disease:

■ diseases of the skeletal, muscular and nervous systems, for example osteoarthritis, muscular dystrophy (also an example of a genetic disease), multiple sclerosis, motor neurone disease and Alzheimer's disease;
■ cardiovascular diseases;
■ cancers.

Cardiovascular diseases (CVDs) are diseases of the circulatory system. They are caused by gradual deterioration of the tissues of the heart and blood vessels. Artery walls become less elastic with age and lose their flexibility. This hardening of the arteries is called **arteriosclerosis** and can be hastened by the deposition of fat in the artery walls. An **atheroma** is a fatty deposit that builds up and makes the lining of the walls rough. The accumulation of fatty material is called **atherosclerosis** and it can cause blood clotting to occur which then blocks the arteries (see page 47). This blood clot is called a **thrombus,** and it can prevent blood flow to surrounding tissues, reducing the supply of oxygen and nutrients so that the tissue cells die.

Box 1A Cancer

Cell division in the body is normally carefully controlled, but cancerous cells lose the ability to respond to the controls and grow into a mass of abnormal cells known as a **tumour**. Most cancers are caused by a combination of genetic and environmental factors. Cancer-causing agents or **carcinogens** are present in the environment and can trigger development of cancer. Asbestos fibres and the tar in tobacco smoke are carcinogens linked with different types of lung cancer. Carcinogens probably cause mutations in the genes, known as **oncogenes**, that control cell division. These mutations can alter the way in which a cell responds to growth factors, causing it to divide uncontrollably.

Tumour cells do not respond to signals from nerves and hormones in the same way as cells in healthy tissues. They continue to grow and fail to undergo programmed cell death. Cancer is not one disease. There are many different types of cancer which occur in nearly every tissue in the body. Some cancers are caused by viruses, for example the human papilloma virus is a cause of cervical cancer.

A small group of tumour cells is called a **primary growth**. There are two types:
1 **benign** tumours, which do not spread from their site of origin, but can compress and displace surrounding tissues, for example warts, ovarian cysts, and growths in fatty tissue (lipomas);
2 **malignant** tumours, which are far more dangerous since they spread throughout the body, invade other tissues and eventually destroy them.

Malignant tumours interfere with the normal functioning of the area where they have started to grow. They may block the intestines, lungs or blood vessels. Cells can break off and spread through the blood and lymphatic system to other parts of the body to form **secondary growths**. The spread of cancers in this way is called **metastasis**. It is the most dangerous characteristic of cancer, since it can be very hard to find secondary cancers and remove them.

SAQ 1.3
Outline the sequence of events that occurs in the development of a cancer.

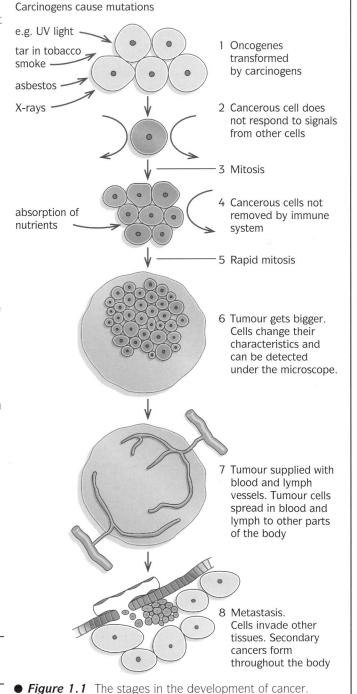

Carcinogens cause mutations

e.g. UV light

tar in tobacco smoke

asbestos

X-rays

1 Oncogenes transformed by carcinogens

2 Cancerous cell does not respond to signals from other cells

3 Mitosis

absorption of nutrients

4 Cancerous cells not removed by immune system

5 Rapid mitosis

6 Tumour gets bigger. Cells change their characteristics and can be detected under the microscope.

7 Tumour supplied with blood and lymph vessels. Tumour cells spread in blood and lymph to other parts of the body

8 Metastasis. Cells invade other tissues. Secondary cancers form throughout the body

● *Figure 1.1* The stages in the development of cancer.

Coronary heart disease (CHD) is a disease of the arteries that supply blood to the heart muscle, causing damage to, or malfunction of, the heart. **Strokes** occur when blood flow to the brain is interrupted by a blockage, or clot, in an artery or when a blood vessel bursts so that there is a leakage of blood into the brain (see chapter 4).

Mental diseases

When brain tissue starts to degenerate, symptoms of mental decline begin. Sufferers, such as those with Parkinson's disease, begin to lose their short-term memory and have difficulty in coordinating and controlling their movements. If untreated they lose control of basic body functions, suffer severe weakness and become incapable of looking after themselves.

The general decline in all mental faculties is called **dementia**. This happens in some degenerative diseases, for example Alzheimer's and Huntington's diseases, and the spongiform encephalopathies such as Creutzfeldt–Jakob disease (CJD). These affect different areas of the brain giving rise to different signs and symptoms. Multiple blockages of blood vessels in the brain due to arteriosclerosis is the most common cause of dementia.

Many mental diseases are not associated with widespread degeneration of the brain. Mild personality disorders are classified as mental disease. These are disorders of the mind affecting thoughts, feelings, emotions and personal and social behaviour.

Mental diseases are categorised into two groups.

1 **Neuroses** or mild disorders, such as anxiety states, for example claustrophobia, agoraphobia and other phobias. These are not associated with any physical malfunction or damage to the brain.
2 **Psychoses**, which are severe disorders that prevent people functioning in a normal manner, for example schizophrenia and manic depression. The causes are unknown, but are likely to be associated with physical damage or a malfunction of neurotransmitters in the brain.

Social diseases

Social factors contribute to the spread of disease. Aspects of the physical environment, such as standards of housing, sanitation, pollution and access to recreational facilities, are important. Social class, poverty and type of occupation can put people at risk of developing certain acute and chronic diseases (e.g. glassblowers and silicosis). Poverty and poor living conditions can encourage disease. For example, infectious diseases tend to spread more easily in overcrowded, insanitary and unhygienic conditions. Obesity and cardiovascular diseases, such as CHD, are more common in affluent countries, but within these countries it is people in the lower socio-economic groups who are afflicted most.

This category of disease can be interpreted very widely to include almost all the infectious diseases and the multifactorial diseases which are influenced by people's living conditions and their personal behaviour.

Self-inflicted diseases

Self-inflicted diseases are those in which people's health is put at risk by their own decisions regarding their behaviour. Those who start smoking at a young age are highly likely to become addicted to nicotine. One study in the UK showed that smoking can kill or cause harm in 24 different ways. For example, it is a major contributory factor to lung cancer, chronic bronchitis, emphysema, high blood pressure and gangrene. Smoking during pregnancy can lead to a mother having an underweight baby. Misusing other drugs, such as alcohol and heroin, can lead to drug dependence, which puts the person at risk of developing a variety of physical and mental diseases (see chapter 7).

Sunbathing can cause blistering of the skin and increases the risk of developing skin cancer. Eating large quantities of fatty food puts people at risk of putting on weight and becoming obese. Deliberate self-harm, such as taking an overdose of tablets in an attempted suicide (parasuicide) could be considered a form of self-inflicted disease. There is often permanent damage to major body organs as a result. In most countries suicide is second only to accidents as a leading cause of death among the young. It is often a response to a sense of hopelessness, failure or frustration.

SAQ 1.4 _____

Make a table to show the classification of the following diseases (each one can be classified into more than one category): scurvy, malaria, measles, cystic fibrosis, lung cancer, sickle cell disease, Parkinson's disease, schizophrenia, Creutzfeldt–Jakob disease and skin cancer.

Epidemiology and patterns of disease distribution

Epidemiology is the study of patterns of disease and the various factors that affect the spread of disease. It is concerned with how diseases affect whole populations, not just individual people. When a new disease appears, as AIDS did in the early 1980s, the cause may not be immediately apparent. Collecting information on the distribution of the disease helps to identify the cause and, if it turns out to be an infectious disease, the way in which it is transmitted. Epidemiology also provides useful information about non-infectious diseases. It was epidemiologists who first identified the link between smoking and lung cancer in the 1950s. They looked for common factors amongst people who developed the disease.

Epidemiologists collect data on the number of people who are ill (**morbidity**) and on the number who have died (**mortality**). This data is always particular to a given population under study, for example that of a city, county or country. To make comparisons between different places or between different years, the data is adjusted in some way. For example, you may find deaths from heart disease expressed as 'per 100 000 population aged between 35 and 64' (see page 45). When data is expressed in this way, fair comparisons can be made which are not possible with simple, unadjusted, death rates.

Three types of data provide information on the spread of disease:

1 *incidence* – the number of new cases in a population occurring per week, month or year;
2 *prevalence* – the number of people in a population with a disease within any given week, month or year;
3 *mortality* – the number of people who have died of a certain disease per week, month or year.

When these three types of data are collected together for all categories of disease they provide good indicators of a nation's health. The World Health Organisation collects such data and identifies common trends so that it can initiate health programmes and coordinate the responses of national health services to changing patterns of disease.

If an infectious disease is always present in a population it is described as being **endemic**. Tuberculosis (TB) is endemic in most parts of the world. Many people have, or have had at some stage, the bacteria in their lungs that cause the disease. They can have the bacteria but not show any symptoms of TB because they have an efficient immune system that prevents the bacteria doing any harm.

An **epidemic** occurs when a disease suddenly spreads rapidly to affect many people. Every few years there are epidemics of influenza that spread across the world. When a disease spreads over a very large area, such as a continent or even the whole world, it is called a **pandemic**. There are pandemics of AIDS and TB at present.

The global distribution of disease often reflects the standards of medical care and affluence in different countries. In developed countries few people have serious infectious diseases and even fewer die from them. Most deaths from disease are due to chronic degenerative diseases which are social and self-inflicted in nature. Improvements in medical technology have not had the same impact on these diseases as they have had on acute, infectious diseases. Reductions in morbidity and mortality from chronic diseases will probably come only from changes in social conditions and people taking positive decisions about their health.

Although the greater proportion of deaths in developing countries occur as a result of infectious diseases this obscures the fact that mortality rate from degenerative diseases is also high.

SUMMARY

- Good health is more than freedom from disease. A healthy person enjoys good mental and physical health and can make a positive contribution to society.

- Disease is a disorder or malfunctioning of the body. Each disease presents a certain set of signs and symptoms.

- Nine different categories of disease are often recognised. Most diseases, however, can be classified into two or more categories.

- Physical diseases are associated with permanent or temporary damage to part of the body. This category includes all the other categories except the less severe mental diseases where there is no sign of any physical damage to the brain.

- Infectious diseases are caused by organisms which parasitise the body. These are viruses, bacteria, fungi, protoctists, worms and insects. Parasites that cause disease are called pathogens.

- Non-infectious diseases are those that are not caused by parasitic organisms.

- Deficiency diseases are caused by the lack of one or more essential nutrients in the diet.

- Inherited diseases are caused by gene or chromosome mutations. Some degenerative diseases are caused by genetic defects. Genes may play an important role in the development of others.

- Degenerative diseases result from a decline in the functions of part of the body. Cancers, diseases of the circulatory system and some inherited and mental diseases (e.g. Huntington's disease) are degenerative diseases.

- Mental diseases are diseases of the mind which may or may not be associated with physical damage to the brain.

- Social diseases are those that are influenced by social conditions such as overcrowding, poverty and people's personal behaviour.

- Self-inflicted diseases are the consequence of people's choices about their behaviour and way of life.

- Epidemiology is the study of disease patterns. Data collected on disease (morbidity) and death (mortality) reveal patterns that can indicate how diseases are spread and their likely cause or causes.

Questions

1 Discuss the statement that health is more than the absence of disease.

2 With reference to named diseases, discuss the problem of classifying diseases into different categories.

3 Explain the differences between the following pairs of categories used to classify diseases: **a** physical and mental, **b** infectious and non-infectious, **c** inherited and deficiency.

4 Explain why cancers are categorised as degenerative diseases.

5 Discuss the factors that influence the differences in prevalence of disease in developed and developing countries.

Chapter two

Diet

By the end of this chapter you should be able to:

1 list the components of a balanced diet;

2 explain what is meant by the term *Dietary Reference Value (DRV)*;

3 describe how DRVs should be used;

4 discuss the relevant quantities of energy and nutrients required by people of both sexes and of different ages and activities;

5 describe the functions of essential amino acids, essential fatty acids and vitamins A and D in the body;

6 discuss the consequences of malnutrition with reference to starvation, protein deficiency, anorexia nervosa, deficiencies of vitamins A and D, and obesity.

A balanced diet

A **balanced diet** is one which provides an adequate intake of energy and nutrients needed for maintenance of the body and thus for good health. We need complex molecules to provide energy for growth, repair, movement and the functioning of our vital organs. Energy is provided by carbohydrates, fats and proteins. We also use these compounds to build the components of cells and tissues. Each day, they are supplied in large quantities in our diet and so are called **macronutrients**. We also need very much smaller quantities of other nutrients, such as vitamins and minerals. These are called **micronutrients**.

Cells can convert some compounds into others; for example glucose can be converted into fat for storage, proteins are synthesised from amino acids, and phospholipids are made from glycerol and fatty acids. However, there are some organic compounds that our cells cannot make from anything else. These compounds have to be provided in our diet. They are:

■ essential amino acids;
■ essential fatty acids;
■ vitamins.

The diet also provides water to replace that which we lose every day, and dietary fibre, material which we cannot digest but which helps move food along the gut by peristalsis, aids good digestion and gives some protection against gut diseases. *Table 2.1* shows the components of a balanced diet and their functions in the body's metabolism.

Individual people require different amounts of the components listed in *Table 2.1*. Additional amounts of proteins, vitamins and minerals are needed for growth, during pregnancy and breast feeding (lactation), and for fighting infections. Height, age, sex, weight, physical activity, the body's basal metabolic rate and even the climate all determine how much food we need. How much we eat is often dictated by other considerations such as cultural, social and economic factors. If our body mass stays constant for several weeks, months or years, then our food intake must equal the demands of our body. If our body mass increases, and no growth is occurring, then our intake exceeds demand. Body mass can also decrease, as it does during starvation. At these times, demand exceeds intake.

Malnutrition results from an unbalanced diet, one in which some nutrients are absent or not in the right quantities to meet our needs. In some cases, too much can be as bad for us as too little. Deficiency diseases are diseases of want, but some diet-related diseases are the result of eating more than we need.

Energy

How much energy do we need? If our body mass stays fairly constant, then we must be eating just the right quantity to meet our needs for growth, metabolism and physical activity. So it is possible to judge how much energy we need by carrying out dietary surveys and asking people what they eat. However, people are not very good at remembering everything they have eaten. Studies suggest

Nutrient	Function
Macronutrients	
carbohydrates	provide energy
fats	provide energy and essential fatty acids
protein	provide essential amino acids for making proteins which have the following functions: structural (e.g. collagen in bone, keratin in hair, actin and myosin in muscle); metabolic (e.g. enzymes); communication (e.g. some hormones); protective (e.g. antibodies); proteins in the diet also provide energy when other stores have run out
Micronutrients	
fat-soluble vitamins:	
A (retinol)	proper functioning of the retina in the eye and epithelial tissues
D	stimulates calcium uptake from the gut and its deposition in bone
E	antioxidant
K	formation in the liver of substances that promote blood clotting
water-soluble vitamins:	
vitamin B complex, including folic acid and B_{12}	respiration, protein synthesis nucleic acid synthesis, red cell production
C	formation of collagen, proper functioning of skin and mucous membranes, antioxidant, stimulates absorption of iron from the gut
minerals:	
calcium	strengthening of bones and teeth; required for muscle contraction
phosphorus	strengthening of bones and teeth; for making ATP, DNA, RNA
iron	haemoglobin, myoglobin, electron carriers in mitochondria
iodine	thyroid hormones
potassium	conduction of nerve impulses, muscle function
sodium	osmotic balance, muscle function, conduction of nerve impulses
chloride	osmotic balance, HCl in stomach
magnesium	development of bones and teeth, enzyme activity
zinc	constituent of some enzymes, involved in wound healing and functioning of insulin
copper, manganese and cobalt	co-factors for enzymes
fluoride	teeth
Dietary fibre (non-starch polysaccharides)	aids peristalsis, prevents constipation
Water	solvent, hydrolysis of food in gut, transport medium (e.g. blood), coolant (sweat), removal of excretory waste in urine

● *Table 2.1* The components of a balanced diet and their functions

that we probably underestimate our food intake by as much as 25%. Surveys of household expenditure (what people buy in the shops) give an indication of the diet of the nation as a whole, but within that there will be much individual variation. *Table 2.2* gives the energy values of the main components of our diet.

It is also possible to estimate energy usage by the technique of calorimetry, which measures how much oxygen is absorbed for respiration. Calorimetry can only be done under laboratory conditions and may not relate very well to everyday life. A new method for estimating energy intake uses isotopes of hydrogen and oxygen as doubly

Nutrient	Energy/kJ g^{-1}
carbohydrate, e.g. glucose, sucrose, lactose, starch	16
fat	37
protein	17
alcohol	29

● **Table 2.2** Energy values of dietary components

labelled water (^{2}H$_2$^{18}O). Breath and urine are sampled for ^{18}O to estimate the rate of carbon dioxide production in respiration. This can be done while people go about their daily lives. Studies like this show that adults need about 8000–9000 kJ of energy every day as a minimum to stay alive.

Dietary Reference Values

Not only is it difficult to find out how much energy we need, it is also not easy to measure the intake of specific nutrients such as proteins and vitamins. Studies on human subjects tend to be difficult and generalisations from animal studies may not be relevant. In 1943, the US Government published **Recommended Dietary Allowances (RDAs)** to help plan diets for military personnel during the Second World War. The first comprehensive set of RDAs (sometimes known as Recommended Daily Allowances or Recommended Daily Amounts) was published in Britain in 1950 and last revised in 1979. In 1991, the British Government's Committee on Medical Aspects of Food Policy (COMA) surveyed all the available data on nutrition and published a revised set of values. The Committee dropped the word 'recommended' since people often mistakenly believed that RDAs were the *minimum* values needed for health. They were not. Most people needed to eat *less than* the RDAs.

The COMA Report introduced the term **Dietary Reference Values (DRVs)** to avoid the suggestion that everyone should be eating the same quantities of nutrients. DRVs reflect the fact that not everyone of the same age needs the same intake of energy or nutrients. Within each age group there is a variation in the food intake required for good health. This is not as a result of poverty or affluence, but as a result of need. For example, two young people of the same age may have different metabolic rates or be growing at different rates.

There are two groups of DRVs. The first group refers to energy and to the nutrients for which COMA found enough data to construct graphs similar to that in *figure 2.1*. The graphs show daily intakes in the diet, and include the following DRVs.

■ *Reference Nutrient Intake (RNI)*
This represents enough, or more than enough, to meet the energy or nutrient needs of almost all the population, even those with high needs. In most cases this is nearly equivalent to the Recommended Daily Amount.
■ *Estimated Average Requirement (EAR)*
This is an estimate of the average requirement of a population: 50% of the population will need more than the EAR for energy or for a nutrient, 50% will need less.
■ *Lower Reference Nutrient Intake (LRNI)*
This is the amount that is sufficient for people with low needs. Most people need more than this.

The RNI and LRNI apply to the nutrients only, as the EAR is the only DRV for energy.

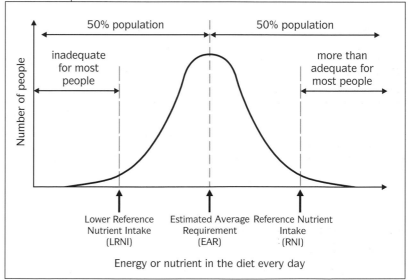

● **Figure 2.1** The requirements for energy and nutrients of a group show a normal distribution. Dietary Reference Values are the three positions indicated on this normal distribution. (RNI and LRNI are two standard deviations above and below the EAR.)

The second group of DRVs are **Safe Intakes**. These are for nutrients (e.g. vitamins E and K, and minerals such as fluoride in children) for which there were insufficient data available to construct graphs similar to *figure 2.1*. An intake below the Safe Intake would risk deficiency; one should aim for an intake just above. However, some micronutrients are toxic in large quantities, so the Safe Intakes are set well below levels that would be unsafe.

As well as varying within any one age group, the requirements for energy and nutrients vary with both age and sex. There are DRVs for males and females of different age groups and for females during pregnancy and lactation (see *tables 2.4, 2.5* and *2.6*. Note that most women only have a requirement for vitamin D during pregnancy and lactation. This explains why vitamin D appears in *table 2.6*, but not in *table 2.5*.)

Calculating EAR for energy

Energy requirements are calculated from basal metabolic rates and the energy needed to support growth and physical activity. The **basal metabolic rate (BMR)** is the energy needed to maintain vital functions such as circulation of the blood, ventilation of the lungs and maintenance of body temperature. Males have a higher BMR than females, partly because they have a higher proportion of muscle, a tissue that has a high metabolic rate. Also, females have a higher proportion of body fat, which provides more insulation, and so they lose less thermal energy per kilogram of body mass than males. *Table 2.3* shows how to calculate BMRs.

EARs are estimated by multiplying the BMR by the **physical activity level (PAL)**, which is the ratio of overall energy use to BMR and is determined by a person's way of life. Therefore:

$$\text{EAR} = \text{BMR} \times \text{PAL}$$

PAL is calculated as follows:

$$\text{PAL} = \frac{\text{total energy required over 24 hours}}{\text{BMR over 24 hours}}$$

A typical PAL for people who take little exercise is 1.4, which applies to most people in the UK. This

Age/years	Calculation of BMR	
	males	females
10 to 17	$0.074M + 2.754$	$0.056M + 2.898$
18 to 29	$0.063M + 2.896$	$0.062M + 2.036$

BMR for 21-year-old male with body mass of 70 kg
$= (0.063 \times 70) + 2.896 = 7.306 \text{ MJ day}^{-1*}$
BMR for 17-year-old female with body mass of 50 kg
$= (0.056 \times 50) + 2.898 = 5.698 \text{ MJ day}^{-1}$

(M = body mass in kg.)

● **Table 2.3** Equations for calculating basal metabolic rates (BMR), in MJ day^{-1}, in 10- to 17-year-olds and 18- to 29-year-olds, with two examples of calculations. *(MJ day^{-1} = megajoules per day. 1 MJ = 1000 kJ.)

represents very little physical activity at work or in leisure time. The EAR is therefore BMR × 1.4. PALs of 1.6 for women and 1.7 for men represent moderate activity during work and leisure; PALs of 1.8 for women and 1.9 for men represent high levels of physical activity.

SAQ 2.1

a Calculate the EARs for energy for
   (i) 17-year-old males who have a body mass of 70 kg at the following PALs – 1.4, 1.7 and 1.9;
   (ii) 20-year-old females who have a body mass of 50 kg at the following PALs – 1.4, 1.6 and 1.8.

b Compare your results with the figures given in *table 2.4* which are for PALs of 1.4.

Age	EAR/MJ day^{-1}	
	males	females
0–3 months (formula fed)	2.28	2.16
4–6 months	2.89	2.69
7–9 months	3.44	3.20
10–12 months	3.85	3.61
1–3 years	5.15	4.86
4–6 years	7.16	6.46
7–10 years	8.24	7.28
11–14 years	9.27	7.92
15–18 years	11.51	8.83
19–49 years	10.60	8.10
50–59 years	10.60	8.00
60–64 years	9.93	7.99

The EARs for adults (over 19 years) given here are based on low activity levels (PAL of 1.4 – see text).

● **Table 2.4** EARs for energy for different age groups and sexes.

SAQ 2.2

Use your results from *SAQ 2.1* to calculate the percentage increase in energy intake with each increase in activity level for the males and the females.

There are no LRNI or RNI values for energy, as individual requirements within each age group vary so much. For example, elite athletes need higher levels than the population average, but the actual energy they need to consume will depend on a variety of factors such as their body mass and training regime. If RNI values were published, some people might eat more than their individual requirement each day, with serious consequences.

SAQ 2.3

Suggest likely outcomes of eating a diet with a daily energy intake greater than required.

SAQ 2.4

Suggest reasons for the variations in RNIs given for different ages for protein, calcium and iron in *table 2.5*.

DRVs for fats and sugars

Energy in the diet is provided by fats, carbohydrates and protein. There is no absolute need for fats in the diet, except for very small quantities of essential fatty acids (see page 17). As the average British diet is alleged to contain high levels of fat and sugar, which are both implicated in diet-related diseases such as heart disease and dental caries, COMA set DRVs for fats and carbohydrates as percentages of total energy intake. In all cases they were less than the average intake of the population. The DRV for total fat intake is 33–35% of total energy intake. In 1994, a survey indicated that in the UK the average food energy derived from fat was 40.5%.

SAQ 2.5

Calculate the mass of fat in a diet that provides 35% of the daily energy intake for 17-year-old males and females.

SAQ 2.6

Explain why reducing fat intake can significantly reduce energy intake.

Age	Protein/ g day^{-1}	Calcium/ mg day^{-1}	Iron/ mg day^{-1}	Zinc/ mg day^{-1}	Vitamin A / µg day^{-1}	Folic acid µg day^{-1}	Vitamin C/ mg day^{-1}
0–3 months*	12.5	525	1.7	4.0	350	50	25
4–6 months	12.7	525	4.3	4.0	350	50	25
7–9 months	13.7	525	7.8	5.0	350	50	25
10–12 months	14.9	525	7.8	5.0	350	50	25
1–3 years	14.5	350	6.9	5.0	400	70	30
4–6 years	19.7	450	6.1	6.5	500	100	30
7–10 years	28.3	550	8.7	7.0	500	150	30
males:							
11–14 years	42.1	1000	11.3	9.0	600	200	35
15–18 years	55.2	1000	11.3	9.5	700	200	40
19–50 years	55.5	700	8.7	9.5	700	200	40
50+ years	53.3	700	8.7	9.5	700	200	40
females:							
11–14 years	41.2	800	14.8	9.0	600	200	35
15–18 years	45.0	800	14.8	7.0	600	200	40
19–50 years	45.0	700	14.8	7.0	600	200	40

*formula fed

● **Table 2.5** Reference Nutrient Intakes (RNIs) for protein and six micronutrients. All the values assume a well-balanced diet in which DRVs for energy and all other nutrients are met. (µg = microgram 1000 µg=1mg)

Fat molecules are composed of fatty acids and glycerol. Fatty acids can be saturated or unsaturated. Saturated fat raises blood cholesterol concentrations (see page 48) and the DRV for it is no more than 10% of total dietary energy. In 1994 the UK population average was 15%. The DRV for starch and the sugars in milk products is 37–39% of total energy intake and for non-milk sugars (e.g. sucrose) it is 10–11%. The COMA Report recommends that no more than 85% of the energy in the diet should come from fats and carbohydrates. Most of the rest will come from protein.

DRVs for fibre

Dietary fibre is provided by polysaccharides such as cellulose, hemicellulose and pectins, found in the cell walls of plants. We do not have enzymes to digest these large, complex compounds so they pass straight through the gut. Fibre does not provide any energy or nutrients, but it gives bulk to food so that peristalsis in the intestines occurs efficiently. Fibre absorbs water and makes sure that some of it is retained when the food reaches the large intestine. This makes it easier to pass faeces and so helps prevent constipation. Fibre may have a protective role in reducing the risk of diseases of the gut. The DRV for fibre in the adult diet is an average of 18 g per day with a range between 12 and 24 g per day.

Water requirements

The daily water turnover in the body is about 4% of the body mass of an adult. Water intake must balance this or else dehydration occurs. Water is needed to replace that lost in the breath, faeces and sweat. It must also supply the kidneys with the minimum amount needed to dissolve all the products of excretion such as urea. Excess water in the body is lost in the urine. The minimum quantity of water needed by a 70 kg male is about 1.5–2.0 dm^3 per day. A cyclist in the Tour de France requires up to 6 dm^3 a day. If there is no water in the diet, death occurs from dehydration within a few days.

SAQ 2.7
State the functions of water in the body.

DRVs for pregnancy and lactation

During pregnancy, a woman's metabolism goes through considerable changes. There is an increase in the metabolic demand to support growth of the uterus, placenta and fetus. This is met by using stores of fat and micronutrients more efficiently than usual. In practice, it is not often necessary to increase the intake of energy significantly until the last three months as pregnant women use fat stores and may be less active than usual. Women who are planning to become pregnant are recommended to supplement their diet with folic acid tablets (400 µg per day) to protect against neural tube defects such as spina bifida in the developing embryo. It is advisable to start supplementing the diet with folic acid before conception since by the time pregnancy is confirmed the embryo may have already developed a neural tube. Other recommended changes are shown in *table 2.6*.

Infants fed on breast milk utilise nutrients very efficiently. Breast milk meets the exact nutritional

Nutrient (DRV)	Pregnancy	Lactation 1st month	Lactation 4 to 6 months
energy (EAR) MJ day^{-1}	+0.8[a]	+1.9	+2.4[b]
protein (RNI) g day^{-1}	+6.0	+11.0	+11.0
calcium (RNI) mg day^{-1}	—	+550	+550
iron (RNI) mg day^{-1}	—	—	—
zinc (RNI) mg day^{-1}	—	+6.0	+2.5
vitamin A (RNI) µg day^{-1}	+100	+350	+350
folic acid (RNI) µg day^{-1}	+100	+60	+60
vitamin C (RNI) mg day^{-1}	+10	+30	+30
vitamin D (RNI) mg day^{-1}	+10	+10	+10

([a] last three months only; [b] if breast milk is infants' main source of energy.)

● **Table 2.6** DRVs for energy and some selected nutrients during pregnancy and lactation. In each case these quantities should be added to a woman's normal intake for her age as given in *tables 2.4* and *2.5*.

needs of a baby including supplying all the energy for growth, development and metabolism. Infants who are fed on formula (powdered) milk do not use nutrients as efficiently. As a result the DRVs for infants fed on formula milk shown in *tables 2.4* and *2.5* give values which are a little higher than the equivalent values for breast milk. There are other advantages of breast feeding; for example, the colostrum produced during the first few days of lactation is rich in antibodies (see page 79).

SAQ 2.8

a   From *table 2.6*, state the EARs for energy for 25-year-old women during pregnancy and during the first and fourth months of lactation.

b   Explain the differences between the EARs for energy during pregnancy and lactation.

c   State the RNIs for the seven micronutrients given in *table 2.6* for 25-year-old women during pregnancy.

d   Explain why women are advised to supplement their diet with folic acid before they become pregnant rather than starting when pregnancy is confirmed.

The uses of Dietary Reference Values

DRVs refer to groups of people; they are not daily recommended quantities for individuals. However, they do provide a guide to the adequacy of individual diets. If you are eating at, or above, the RNI for nutrients (e.g. protein, iron and vitamin A), then it is unlikely that you are deficient in these nutrients since so few people in the population have very high requirements (*figure 2.1*). No harm is done by eating just above the RNI values. The EARs for energy show the average energy intake for the population; but there may be many reasons for people having intakes above or below the EAR, which is just a guide to how much food energy people require. Harm is done if energy intake exceeds the daily requirement.

DRVs are useful in assessing information from dietary surveys, especially if it is suspected that a population is suffering from a dietary disease such as anaemia. For example, a survey of the nutrition of young children in the UK (published in 1995) found that 84% of those under four years old were consuming less than the RNI for iron (6.9 mg a day). As many as 16% were consuming less than the LRNI (3.7 mg a day).

SAQ 2.9

Suggest why there is concern about iron deficiency in children.

Box 2A Food labels

Food manufacturers may print nutritional information on packets of food. If they do so then the information must be presented in a standard form. As a result of the 1996 Food Labelling Regulations, any food manufacturer in the United Kingdom who declares that a food is a source of a micronutrient, such as vitamin C or folic acid, must show on the label that a normal daily serving of the food supplies at least 17% of the Recommended Daily Allowance for food labelling. If a manufacturer claims that the food is a rich source (eg. rich in vitamin C),the label must then show that a normal daily serving supplies at least 50% of the RDA. This explains why you will find RDAs given on labels for foods such as breakfast cereals and fruit juices.

RDAs for food labelling were introduced by European Directive 90/496 and differ from the DRVs published by COMA in 1991. For example, the RNI for vitamin C for adults is 40 mg, the European RDA is 60 mg. The RDAs apply to adults and the quantities are sufficient for the needs of the population as a whole. The figures *(table 2.7)* are derived from World Health Organisation recommendations.

The nutritional contents of fresh or dry produce that is not sold in packets can be found by consulting tables such as those published by the Ministry of Agriculture, Fisheries and Food (see their *Manual of Nutrition*).

Micronutrient	*Recommended daily allowance*
vitamin A	800 µg
vitamin B₁	1.4 mg
vitamin C	60 mg
vitamin D	5 µg
folic acid	200 µg
calcium	800 mg
iron	14 mg
zinc	15 mg

● **Table 2.7** The recommended daily allowances for eight of the micronutrients for which regulations governing food labels exist in the UK

As DRVs apply to groups of people, they are useful for caterers and dietitians devising meals for institutions such as hospitals, schools, military bases, prisons and old people's homes. However, DRVs cannot be used to assess the dietary requirements of people suffering from diseases which affect the absorption or use of nutrients. For example in disorders of the gut many nutrients may not be absorbed and people with such disorders will need higher levels than the RNIs.

Proteins and essential amino acids

Proteins fulfill a variety of roles in the body *(table 2.1)*. All are synthesised inside the cells from amino acids. There are twenty different amino acids, all with the same basic structure but with different **R groups** (see *Foundation Biology*, pages 41 and 88). It is surprising, considering the importance of amino acids, that humans (and most other vertebrates) can synthesise only just over half of the amino acids from simpler compounds. We can make eight of them from compounds involved in glycolysis and the Krebs cycle. These are the non-essential amino acids; for example, alanine is made from pyruvate; glutamate, glutamine and proline are made from oxaloacetate (a Krebs cycle intermediate). Pyruvate and the Krebs cycle intermediates are 'carbon skeletons' to which the amino group ($-NH_2$) is added to make amino acids. We cannot make carbon skeletons for the remaining twelve amino acids. Eight of these are the **essential amino acids (EAAs)**, which must be supplied in the diet as we cannot make proteins without them *(table 2.8)*.

Some of the essential amino acids are used to make non-essential amino acids. For example, phenylalanine is converted into tyrosine; methionine is converted into cysteine. If the diet is deficient in these two essential amino acids, then tyrosine and cysteine may also be deficient unless they are supplied in the diet.

Cells draw upon a pool of amino acids for protein synthesis. Amino acids brought to cells by the blood come from two sources:

- dietary protein digested and absorbed in the gut;
- breakdown of body protein (e.g. muscle).

Ageing cells and organelles are constantly renewed even when growth is finished. Proteins are constantly broken down and rebuilt. Dietary protein adds a supply of amino acids to 'top up' the pool. However, unlike fats and carbohydrates, there is no store of amino acids for cells to draw on. Any amino acids in excess of immediate requirements are broken down. The $-NH_2$ groups released are used for the synthesis of non-essential amino acids or are converted into urea and

Essential amino acid	*Estimated daily amino acid requirements/$mg\,kg^{-1}$ body mass day^{-1}*			
	infants *3–4 months*	*children* *2 years old*	*boys* *10–12 years*	*adults*
histidine	28	?	?	8–12
isoleucine	70	31	28	10
leucine	161	73	44	14
lysine	103	64	44	12
methionine (+ cysteine)	58	27	22	13
phenylalanine (+ tyrosine)	125	69	22	14
threonine	87	37	28	7
tryptophan	17	12	3	3
valine	93	38	25	10
Totals	742	351	216	91–95

Cysteine and tyrosine are required in the diet if methionine and phenylalanine are in short supply. Children cannot make histidine fast enough for growth; adults can make enough for their requirements. The eight essential acids required by adults are shown in bold.

● *Table 2.8* Estimates of daily essential amino acid requirements.

excreted. The rest of the molecules (the carbon skeletons) are respired or converted into fat and stored. It is therefore important to maintain the dietary intake of protein every day, although the body can make adjustments if there is a deficiency (see page 20).

Almost every human protein contains all the essential amino acids. If any are deficient, proteins cannot be made. Some foods contain all the essential amino acids in sufficient quantities to meet the needs of a child or an adult. It is not surprising that these foods are of animal origin, as animal tissues have similar proteins to our own. Some protein foods do not supply the full range of EAAs. The amino acid which is present in the smallest quantity in a food is described as the **limiting amino acid** for that food. The limiting amino acids of milk, eggs and beef are not EAAs; wheat, however, is deficient in lysine, maize in tryptophan and soya beans in methionine. A limiting EAA can easily be made up by supplementing the diet or by eating a mixture of protein foods; for example, cheese supplies the lysine that is deficient in bread.

There are no DRVs for individual amino acids as the British diet usually contains enough protein to supply all the EAAs in sufficient quantities. This is not the case in the developing world where the diet may not contain enough protein. In 1985 the Food and Agriculture Organisation and the World Health Organisation suggested target values of EAAs for adults and infants. These are shown in *table 2.8*. Vegans do not eat any food of animal origin, but if their diets contain a wide selection of plant foods they can obtain all the EAAs and micronutrients they need except vitamin B_{12}.

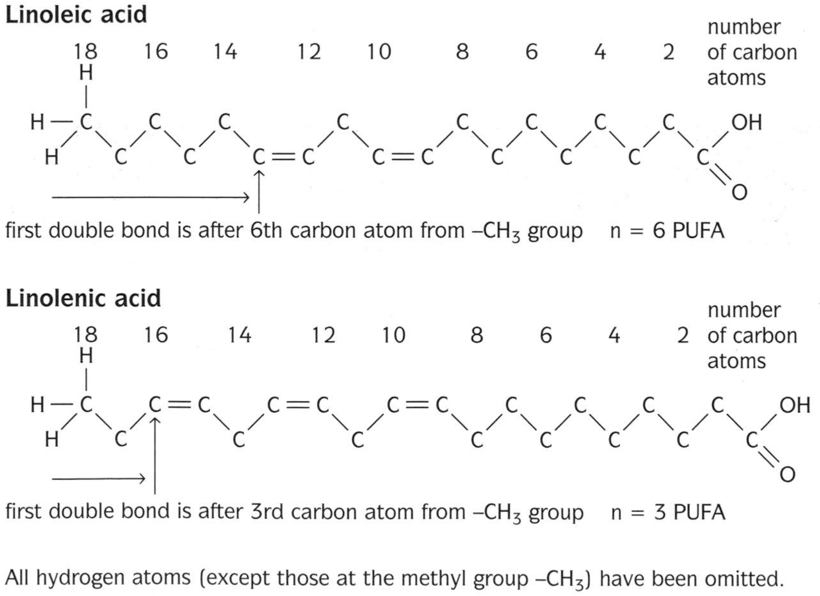

Linoleic acid

first double bond is after 6th carbon atom from $-CH_3$ group   n = 6 PUFA

Linolenic acid

first double bond is after 3rd carbon atom from $-CH_3$ group   n = 3 PUFA

All hydrogen atoms (except those at the methyl group $-CH_3$) have been omitted.

● **Figure 2.2** The chemical structure of the two essential polyunsaturated fatty acids (PUFAs): linoleic and linolenic acids. Vegetable oils such as soya, sunflower and maize are rich in them.

SAQ 2.10
Suggest the likely effects of eating a diet deficient in essential amino acids.

SAQ 2.11
Make a list of the types of plant foods that should be included in a vegan diet.

Essential fatty acids

Fatty acids are long chain hydrocarbon molecules present in the diet as components of fats and oils known as triglycerides. Fats and oils are compounds of glycerol and three fatty acids. Oils have a lower melting point than fats and are liquids at room temperature.

Fatty acids are classified according to the number of double bonds they have. Saturated fatty acids have none; monounsaturated fatty acids have one, polyunsaturated fatty acids (PUFAs) have two or more (see *Foundation Biology*, page 40). Some PUFAs are essential nutrients since they cannot be synthesised in the body from anything else. This is because we do not have the enzyme for introducing double bonds beyond carbon atom 9 in a hydrocarbon chain (*figure 2.2*).

The essential fatty acids (EFAs) are linoleic and linolenic acids. These are needed for the formation of cell membrane phospholipids. The liver converts linoleic acid into arachidonic acid, which is transported to other tissues and stored in the lipid bilayer of cell membranes. Arachidonic acid is converted into the hormone-like prostaglandins and thromboxanes, which play important signalling roles in the renal, immune and circulatory systems (see page 48). We need very small quantities of EFAs in the diet. Well-nourished people probably have a year's supply in their fat stores. The DRVs for linoleic acid and linolenic acid are 1% and 0.2% of total energy intake respectively. Most British diets probably provide 8–15 g of EFAs a day. Deficiencies of EFAs cause limited growth in infants, scaly skin, hair loss and poor wound healing. The intake, by men who have suffered a heart attack, of long-chain n-3 PUFAs with 20 to 22 carbon atoms and three double bonds reduces the risk of further attacks. Oily fish such as mackerel are rich in these PUFAs.

Vitamins

Vitamins are compounds which the body cannot synthesise, so they must be in the diet. They do not share the same molecular structure, unlike the EAAs and the EFAs, and they are required in trace quantities. Vitamins carry out a variety of functions (*table 2.1*) and prevent specific deficiency diseases. The RNIs for vitamins A and C are given in *table 2.5*.

Vitamin A

Vitamin A, or retinol, is not widely distributed in food. It is in some animal foods, such as milk, eggs, liver and fish-liver oils as well as in some fruit (mango and papaya). Related compounds, such as carotenoids (e.g. β carotene), are in a wide variety of vegetables such as cabbage, carrots and spinach. β carotene is converted in the body into retinol. In well-nourished people the liver stores enough vitamin A to last one or two years. It is stored in the liver because in high blood concentrations the vitamin is toxic.

Children with vitamin A deficiency often have dry, rough skin, inflammation of the eyes, a drying or scarring of the cornea (**xerophthalmia** – see *figure 2.3*) and cannot see in dim light (**night blindness**). Rod cells in the retina of the eye detect light of low intensity, for example in late evening and at night. They convert vitamin A into a pigment, rhodopsin, which is bleached when light enters the eye. Rod cells resynthesise rhodopsin, but if there

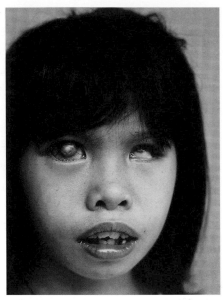

● *Figure 2.3* This girl from Thailand is blind from scarring of the cornea as a result of Vitamin A deficiency.

is a deficiency of the vitamin, rod cells can no longer function and night blindness is the result.

Epithelial cells use retinol to make retinoic acid, an intracellular messenger used in cell differentiation and growth. Without retinoic acid epithelia are not maintained properly and the body becomes susceptible to infections, particularly measles and infections of the respiratory system and gut.

Children who are fed diets based mainly on cereals (maize, rice or wheat) with small quantities of meat or fresh vegetables are at risk of vitamin A deficiency, which is thought to be responsible for half a million cases of childhood blindness worldwide (40–50% of the total). Millions more children receive just enough vitamin A to stave off blindness but not enough to maintain either their immune system or their epithelia.

Vitamin D

This is sometimes known as the 'sunshine vitamin'. If the skin receives sufficient sunlight then the body can make enough vitamin D, so it is not really needed in the diet. Even though many people in Britain do not receive much sunlight in the winter, the amount made in the summer months (mainly between May and July) is enough to last the rest of the year because Vitamin D is stored in muscles and fat. The RNI for people confined indoors and for those whose religion requires them to wear completely enveloping clothes is 10 µg per day. Dark skin produces little vitamin D, so dark-skinned people in temperate countries must also ensure that they receive enough vitamin D in their diet. Foods such as eggs and oily fish are rich in vitamin D, and margarine and low fat spreads are fortified with it. Supplements are available for children and pregnant and lactating women.

Enzymes in the liver and kidney convert vitamin D into an active form (known as 'active vitamin D') which acts as a hormone to stimulate epithelial cells in the intestine to absorb calcium. It does this by entering the cells and activating the genes responsible for the production of a calcium-binding substance, calbindin. This mode of action is typical of steroid hormones, of which vitamin D is one.

Vitamin D also acts on bone cells to regulate the deposition of calcium. A deficiency of vitamin D in children leads to rickets (*figure 2.4*). In adults it causes **osteomalacia**, a progressive softening which makes the bones susceptible to fracture. Women, especially in developing countries, who have a number of children and breast-feed them are at risk of developing osteomalacia.

SAQ. 2.12

A study in Holland during the Second World War showed that nuns were particularly susceptible to osteomalacia. Suggest why this was so.

SAQ. 2.13

Suggest which groups of people in the UK are most at risk of rickets and osteomalacia.

Starvation

A shortage or complete lack of food leads to starvation. During starvation, or semi-starvation, the body adapts by reducing the

Kwashiorkor	*Marasmus*
underweight	very underweight
oedema	no oedema
'moon face'	'old man's face'
muscle wasting	muscle wasting
dry, brittle and thin, reddish hair	little change to hair
fatty enlarged liver	little fat
bloated appearance	wrinkled skin
apathetic	mentally alert
loss of appetite	no loss of appetite

● **Table 2.9** The features of kwashiorkor and marasmus. Children with marasmus probably adapt better to a shortage of energy than those with kwashiorkor.

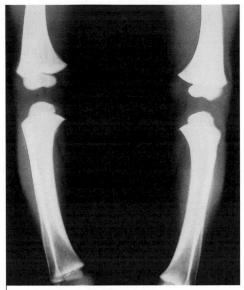

● **Figure 2.4** An X-ray of weakened bones and bowed legs of a child with rickets. The long bones are severely deformed because they lack the strengthening that calcium salts provide.

basal metabolic rate (BMR). Some people have survived for up to 70 days without food, so long as they have access to water, because they use their resources of carbohydrate, fat and protein to provide energy. People who were well fed before starvation began often do not suffer from any micronutrient deficiencies as most of them are stored in the body. Those on a poor diet before starvation may well show symptoms, particularly those of vitamin A deficiency. Both groups suffer from energy malnutrition, sometimes called **protein energy malnutrition (PEM)**. The worst form of this is seen in young children, especially when they are weaned onto poor, starchy foods. Such children grow slowly and have high mortality rates. Two extreme forms of PEM are **kwashiorkor** and **marasmus** (see *figure 2.5* and *table 2.9*).

● *Figure 2.5* The wizened expression, muscle wasting and wrinkled dry skin of this boy are characteristic of marasmus, a form of protein energy malnutrition.

As starvation proceeds the body adapts by using:

■ glycogen stores in the liver (these last less than a day);

■ fat stores (lasting between four and six weeks, depending on the amount stored, the physical activity and the temperature);

■ protein in muscles and other tissue (lasting between one and two weeks).

At first the body probably protects its protein supplies and respires mostly fat. In kwashiorkor there is a shortage of protein and few plasma proteins are made. This increases the water potential of the blood, so the tissues start to swell with water. The characteristic bloated abdomen of a child with kwashiorkor is a result of a swollen liver and the accumulation of fluid in the tissues, a condition known as **oedema**. More common symptoms of PEM are the conditions of wasting and stunting.

■ *Wasting* is characteristic of acute PEM as there is rapid weight loss or a failure to put on weight.

■ *Stunting* is characteristic of chronic PEM as there is an inability to grow in height. This is difficult to reverse because it is often caused by prolonged malnutrition over a long time.

It used to be thought that these symptoms were caused only by a lack of protein and that they could be reversed with a very protein-rich diet. This probably did more harm than good. People recovering from starvation need about 8% of the energy they consume as protein. Cereals, such as maize and wheat, contain 8–11%. What malnourished people therefore require is an increase in staple foods and intake of energy. As food quantity increases, protein content increases in proportion. Unimix is an example of a food used in emergency feeding programmes in famine areas in the developing world *(table 2.10)*. Supplementary feeding *(figure 2.6)* may be required if diets do not provide enough micronutrients, as during famines when children

● *Figure 2.6* Supplementary feeding provided by World Vision at Almata, Wollo Province, during the Ethiopian famine of 1986. Aid organisations not only provide emergency feeding during famines, but also run long-term programmes in agriculture, nutrition and health to ensure people have secure supplies of food.

Nutrient	Mass per 100 g Unimix
protein	6.82 g
fat	21.80 g
carbohydrate	62.50 g
calcium	92.4 mg
phosphorus	113.10 mg
iron	3.08 mg
potassium	145.8 mg
vitamin A	231.0 µg
vitamin B_1	0.39 mg
vitamin B_2	0.23 mg
vitamin B_3	3.17 mg

● *Table 2.10* Nutritional value per 100 g (dry mass) of 'Unimix'. Each child receives about 350 g per day.

suffer from nutritional deficiencies. Children fed on starchy root crops such as cassava, which contains only about 2% protein, should also be given supplementary protein.

SAQ. 2.14

a From *tables 2.2* and *2.10*, calculate the total energy content in a day's supply of Unimix

b Compare the result with the EARs for energy for children of different ages as given in *table 2.4*

c Compare the daily provision of protein, iron, calcium and vitamin A in Unimix with the RNIs given in *table 2.5* for children between one and ten years of age.

In most developed countries, even among the poorest of the population, there is rarely a problem with insufficient energy intakes. One exception is during or immediately after a prolonged war *(figure 2.7)*. A few people do have problems with digestion and absorption of food, or specific nutrient deficiencies such as anaemia. There is also the eating disorder, anorexia nervosa.

SAQ. 2.15

During the famine in the Netherlands in 1945, women tended to survive for several weeks longer than men. Suggest a reason for this.

Anorexia nervosa

Anorexia nervosa is a wasting disease brought on by psychological distress. Most anorexics are teenagers, and 90% of diagnosed cases are female. The causes are probably complex, but most have to do with anxiety over growing up, sexuality and poor self-image or low self-esteem. Up to half of girls and a third of boys responding to surveys in Britain say that they are concerned about their body image. Many girls admire the 'supermodels' (sometimes called 'superwaifs') and attempt to emulate them.

Anorexia develops from reducing weight by dieting. Even anorexics who have lost a considerable amount of weight consider themselves to be too fat. They become obsessive about food and eat less and less. They resist the pangs of hunger and may be obsessed with diet, exercise and death. The disease is the physiological equivalent of marasmus in younger children. Symptoms include muscle wasting (including heart muscle), loss of body fat, thin sparse hair, cold hands and feet and low blood pressure *(figure 2.8)*. There is limited sexual development and the normal menstrual cycle stops resulting in infertility. Anorexics are highly susceptible to infections and they may lose so much weight that they die of starvation.

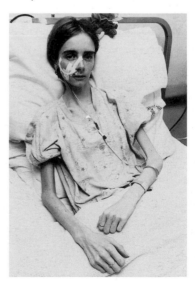

● *Figure 2.8* An anorexic girl. When weight falls below 75% of an acceptable level, anorexics are often admitted to a hospital or clinic to establish a normal eating pattern. Psychological support is often given. Some may have to be force fed.

● *Figure 2.7* These children photographed in Amsterdam in 1945 survived the famine in Holland caused by the disruption at the end of the Second World War and severe flooding. Over one thousand people died in the city, and many more in the rest of the Netherlands.

Obesity

Overeating is a form of malnutrition. Food that is eaten in excess of that required is stored as fat. Obesity *(figure 2.9)* is the most prevalent form of malnutrition in affluent countries and is associated with a high fat intake in the diet, and lack of exercise. It increases the risk of developing the following diseases: diabetes, hypertension, coronary heart disease, arthritis, cancer (especially of colon, rectum and prostate in men and uterus, cervix and breast in women), and stroke. It also increases the likelihood of developing hernia, varicose veins and gallstones. Surgical operations carry a greater risk in people who are obese.

Obesity is defined in two ways:

1 20% or more above the recommended weight for height; or
2 a body mass index of greater than 30.

The body mass index (BMI) is calculated as:

$$\text{Body mass index} = \frac{\text{body mass (in kg)}}{\text{height (in metres)}^2}$$

A man of 1.73 m (5'8") who is 70 kg has a BMI of 23. This falls in the 'acceptable' category *(table 2.11)*, but samples of the population since 1980 show an increase in the percentage of people who are overweight and obese in the UK *(table 2.12)*.

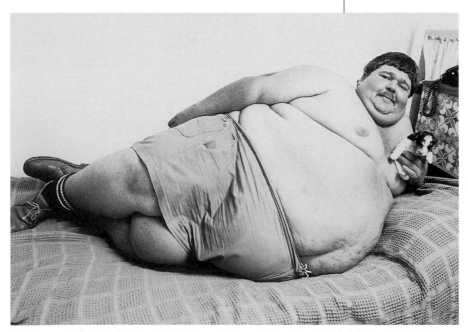

● *Figure 2.9* An obese man. He aims to keep his body mass at 120 kg (19 stone).

BMI	Category
< 20	underweight
20–24	acceptable
25–30	overweight
>30	obese

● *Table 2.11* Body mass indices

	1980	*1986/87*	*1991/92*	*1993*
		Percentage of sample		
Men				
Obese	6	7	13	13
Overweight	33	38	40	43
Acceptable	51	49	41	39
Underweight	10	6	6	5
Total	100	100	100	100
Women				
Obese	8	12	15	16
Overweight	24	24	26	30
Acceptable	54	53	50	46
Underweight	14	11	9	8
Total	100	100	100	100

● *Table 2.12* Samples of the population since 1980 showing an increase in the percentage of people who are overweight and obese in the UK.

SAQ 2.16

Three people have the following heights: 1.65 metres (5'5"), 1.73 m (5'8") and 1.83 m (6'0"). They each have a BMI of 30. Calculate their individual body masses.

Taking measurements of waistbands is far easier than calculating the BMI. One long-term investigation showed that women with waists greater than 80 cm (31.4 inches) and men with waists greater than 94 cm (36.9 inches) were twice as likely to develop cardiovascular diseases than the rest of the population. The waist to hip ratio indicates where most fat is deposited. Studies show that men with a high ratio are at a greater risk of cardiovascular diseases and diabetes. Most of their fat is deposited around the waist (the 'apple shape') rather than around the hips ('pear shape') as in women. However, women with fat distributed in the 'apple shape' have the same risk of developing serious disease as men of that shape.

SUMMARY

A balanced diet must provide: sufficient energy for basal metabolic rate, growth and physical activity; essential amino acids and essential fatty acids; micronutrients: vitamins and minerals; water and fibre.

Dietary Reference Values (DRVs) describe the required energy and nutrient intakes of the British population. When plotted on a graph these intakes show a normal distribution. The Estimated Average Requirement (EAR) is the population average, the Reference Nutrient Intake (RNI) is a value that covers most of the population; the Lower Reference Nutrient Intake (LRNI) provides enough for only a very small proportion of the population. These values provide useful standards for analysing dietary surveys and for planning diets for groups of people.

The DRV for energy is the EAR. The DRVs for protein and most of the micronutrients are EARs, RNIs and LRNIs. Safe Intakes are the DRVs for two vitamins (E and K) and several minerals (e.g. fluoride).

Essential amino acids are required for protein synthesis; essential fatty acids are required for making phospholipids and for specific compounds required for signalling between cells.

Vitamin A is needed for proper functioning of the retina and epithelia; vitamin D is needed for bone growth and development.

Malnutrition is any disorder of nutrition resulting from eating an unbalanced diet. Starvation is caused by a lack of food and leads to exhaustion of body reserves of carbohydrate, fat and protein. Marasmus, kwashiorkor and anorexia nervosa are forms of protein energy malnutrition.

Specific deficiency diseases, for example rickets, occur when there are micronutrient deficiencies.

Overeating is a form of malnutrition which can lead to obesity and increase the risk of developing many diseases such as cardiovascular disease and diabetes.

Questions

1 **a** Explain the term *balanced diet*. **b** Discuss the importance of diet in preventing disease.

2 Explain the term *Dietary Reference Values* and discuss the advantages of publishing these values for energy, protein and micronutrients.

3 Describe and explain the dietary advice that a nutritionist might give to the following groups of people: **a** pregnant women, **b** elite athletes, **c** the elderly, **d** Arctic explorers.

4 Discuss the functions of the following in the body: **a** essential amino acids, **b** essential fatty acids, **c** vitamin A, **d** vitamin D.

5 Discuss the impact of malnutrition on developed and developing countries.

6 Describe the health risks of anorexia nervosa and obesity.

Gaseous exchange and exercise

1 interpret photographs and drawings of lung tissue to show distribution of alveoli and blood vessels;

2 interpret photographs and drawings of the trachea to show the distribution of cartilage, ciliated epithelium, goblet cells and smooth muscle;

3 describe the functions of cartilage, cilia, goblet cells, smooth muscle and elastic fibres in the gaseous exchange system;

4 explain the meanings of the terms *tidal volume* and *vital capacity*;

5 understand that pulse rate is a measure of heart rate and explain the significance of resting pulse rate in relation to physical fitness;

6 explain the terms *systolic blood pressure*, *diastolic blood pressure* and *hypertension*;

7 describe the immediate effects of exercise on the body, including the concept of oxygen debt and the production of lactate by anaerobic respiration;

8 explain the meaning of the term *aerobic exercise*;

9 describe how much exercise needs to be taken for significant sustained improvement in aerobic fitness;

10 discuss the long-term consequences of exercise on the body and the benefits of maintaining a physically fit body, relating these benefits to the concept that health is more than the absence of disease.

The gaseous exchange system

The gaseous exchange system links the circulatory system with the atmosphere. It is adapted to:

■ clean and warm the air that enters;
■ maximise the surface area for diffusion;
■ minimise the distance for diffusion of oxygen and carbon dioxide.

Lungs

The lungs are the site of gaseous exchange between air and blood and they present a huge surface area to the air that flows in and out. They are in the thoracic (chest) cavity surrounded by an airtight space between the pleural membranes. This space contains a small quantity of fluid to allow friction-free movement as the lungs are ventilated by the movement of the diaphragm and ribs.

Trachea, bronchi and bronchioles

The lungs are ventilated with air which passes through a branching system of airways (*figure 3.1* and *table 3.1*). Leading from the throat to the lungs is the **trachea**. At the base of the trachea are two **bronchi** (singular **bronchus**), which subdivide and branch extensively forming a bronchial 'tree' in each lung. **Cartilage** in the trachea and bronchi keep these airways open and air resistance low, and prevents them from collapsing or bursting as the air pressure changes during breathing. In the trachea there is a regular arrangement of C-shaped rings of

Airway	Number	Diameter	Cartilage	Goblet cells	Smooth muscle	Cilia	Site of gas exchange
trachea	1	1.8 cm	yes	yes	yes	yes	no
bronchus	2	1.2 cm	yes	yes	yes	yes	no
terminal bronchiole	48 000	1.0 mm	no	no	yes	yes	no
respiratory bronchiole	300 000	0.5 mm	no	no	no	yes	no
alveolar duct	9×10^6	400 µm	no	no	no	no	yes
alveoli	3×10^9	250 µm	no	no	no	no	yes

● **Table 3.1** The structure of the airways from the trachea to the alveoli. The parts of the airways are shown in *figure 3.1*

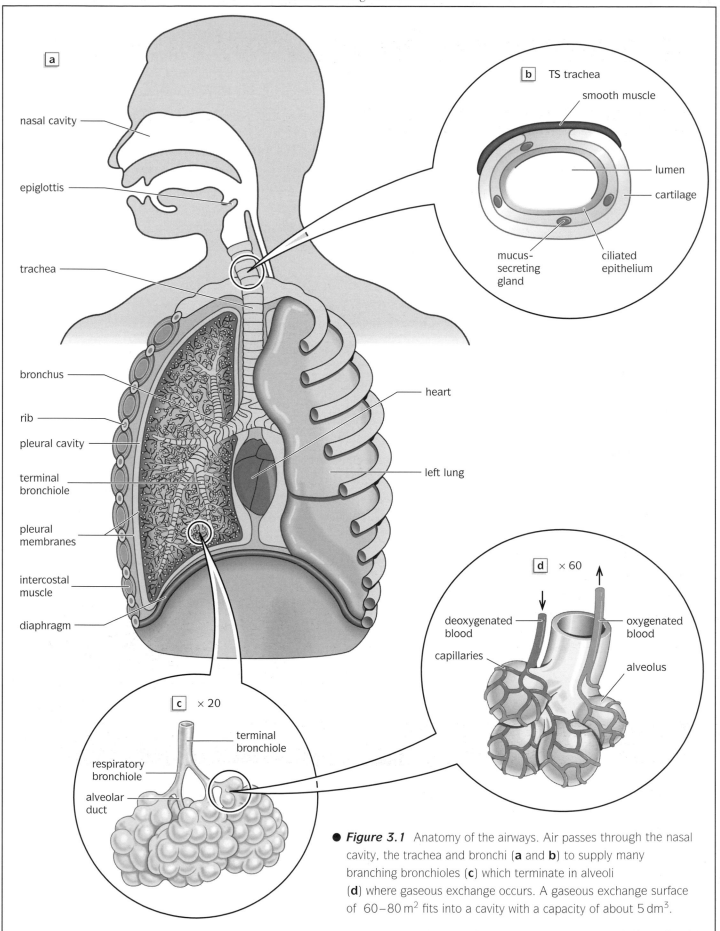

a

nasal cavity

epiglottis

trachea

bronchus

rib

pleural cavity

terminal bronchiole

pleural membranes

intercostal muscle

diaphragm

heart

left lung

b TS trachea

smooth muscle

lumen

cartilage

mucus-secreting gland

ciliated epithelium

d × 60

deoxygenated blood

oxygenated blood

capillaries

alveolus

c × 20

terminal bronchiole

respiratory bronchiole

alveolar duct

● **Figure 3.1** Anatomy of the airways. Air passes through the nasal cavity, the trachea and bronchi (**a** and **b**) to supply many branching bronchioles (**c**) which terminate in alveoli (**d**) where gaseous exchange occurs. A gaseous exchange surface of 60–80 m^2 fits into a cavity with a capacity of about 5 dm^3.

cartilage; in the bronchi there are irregular blocks of cartilage instead. The small bronchioles are surrounded by smooth muscle which can contract or relax to adjust the diameter of these tiny airways. During exercise they relax to allow a greater flow of air to the alveoli. The absence of cartilage makes these adjustments possible.

Warming and cleaning the air

As air flows through the nose and the trachea it is warmed to body temperature and moistened by evaporation from the moist lining, so protecting the delicate surfaces inside the lungs from desiccation. Protection is also needed against

the suspended matter carried in the air, which may include dust, pollen, bacteria, fungal spores, sand and viruses. All are a potential threat to the proper functioning of the lungs. Particles larger than about 5–10 μm are caught on the hairs inside the nose and the **mucus** lining the nasal passages and other airways.

In the trachea and bronchi, the mucus is produced by the **goblet cells** of the ciliated epithelium (*figures 3.2 and 3.3*). In *figure 3.3* the epithelium looks as if it is made of separate layers of cells, but this is deceptive. Each cell reaches the basement membrane and so it is a pseudostratified epithelium. The upper part of each goblet cell is swollen with droplets containing **mucin** which have been secreted by the cell. The rest of the cell, which contains the nucleus, is quite slender like the stem of a goblet. Mucus is also made by glands beneath the epithelium (*figure 3.1b*). Mucus is a slimy solution of mucin, which is composed of glycoproteins with many carbohydrate chains to make them sticky and trap particles in inhaled air. Some chemicals, such as sulphur dioxide and nitrogen dioxide, dissolve in mucus to form an acid solution which can irritate the lining of the airways.

Between the goblet cells are the ciliated cells. The continual beating of their cilia carries the carpet of mucus upwards towards the larynx. Each cilium has a tiny hook at the end to sweep the mucus, which moves at a speed of about 1 cm per minute. When mucus reaches the top of the trachea it is usually swallowed so that pathogens are destroyed by the acid in the stomach.

Phagocytic white blood cells known as **macrophages** patrol the surfaces of the airways scavenging small particles such as bacteria and fine dust particles. During an infection they are joined by other phagocytic cells which leave the capillaries to help remove pathogens.

● *Figure 3.2* Scanning electron micrograph of the surface of the trachea, showing large numbers of cilia and some mucus-secreting goblet cells. The cilia sweep mucus and the debris it collects towards the larynx. This 'mucociliary escalator' sweeps potentially harmful substances away from the delicate alveoli. (× 2000)

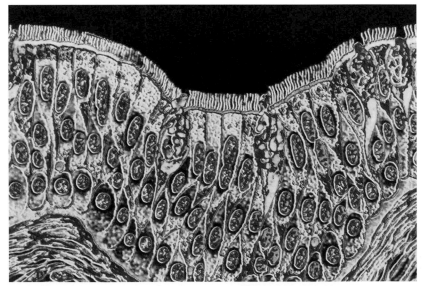

● *Figure 3.3* A transverse section of the ciliated epithelium of the trachea showing several mucus-secreting goblet cells. (× 1000)

Alveoli

At the end of the pathway between the atmosphere and the bloodstream are the **alveoli** (*figures 3.4* and *3.5*). These have a very thin epithelial lining and are surrounded by many blood capillaries carrying deoxygenated blood. The short distance between air and blood means that oxygen and carbon dioxide can be exchanged efficiently by diffusion. Alveolar walls contain **elastic fibres** which stretch during breathing and recoil during expiration to help force out air. This elasticity allows alveoli to expand according to the volume of air breathed in. When fully expanded during exercise the surface area available for diffusion increases, and the air is expelled efficiently when the elastic fibres recoil.

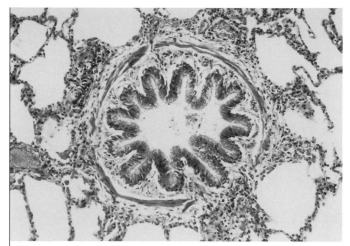

● **Figure 3.4** A photomicrograph of a small bronchiole surrounded by alveoli. Compare this photograph with *figure 3.5a*. (× 100)

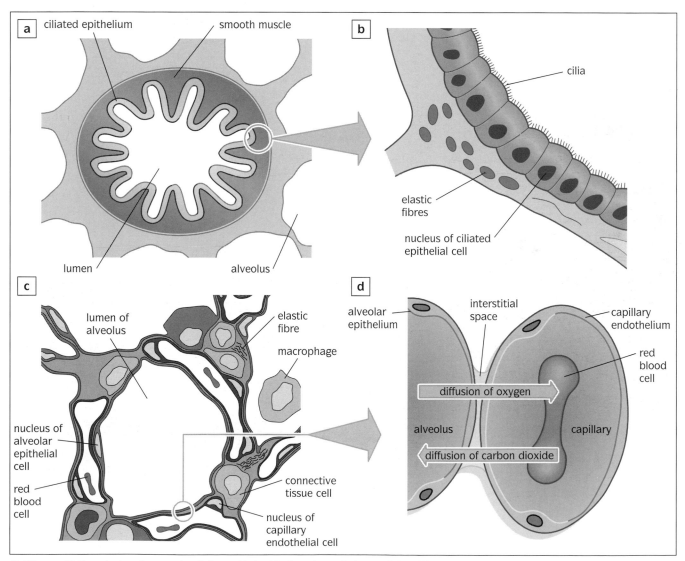

● **Figure 3.5** **a** A drawing made of *figure 3.4* with **b** enlarged views of the ciliated epithelium, **c** an alveolus and **d** the barrier between air in an alveolus and blood in a capillary.

SAQ 3.1 _____

Describe the pathway taken by a molecule of oxygen as it passes from the atmosphere to the blood in the lungs.

SAQ 3.2 _____

Explain how alveoli are adapted for gaseous exchange.

SAQ 3.3 _____

Explain the advantage of being able to adjust the diameter of bronchioles.

Breathing and exercise

Breathing refreshes the air in the alveoli so that the concentrations of oxygen and carbon dioxide within them remain constant. Changing the depth and rate of breathing achieves this. At rest we need to ventilate our lungs with about $6.0\,dm^3$ of air per minute. About $0.35\,dm^3$ of air enters the alveoli with each breath, representing only about one seventh of the total volume of air in the alveoli. This means that large changes in the composition of alveolar air never occur. In any case, it is impossible to empty the lungs completely, and even when the chest is compressed during forced exhalation, about $1.0\,dm^3$ of air still remains in the alveoli and the airways. This volume is the **residual volume**. A much larger volume (approximately $2.5\,dm^3$) remains in the lungs after breathing out normally. When breathing deeply the lungs can increase in volume by as much as $3\,dm^3$.

As exercise becomes harder the depth of breathing increases and often the breathing rate does too. This gives us the ability to respond to changes in demand for gaseous exchange during exercise. The effect of exercise on breathing is measured by calculating the **ventilation rate** (see box 3A). This is the total volume of air moved into the lungs in one minute. Ventilation rate (expressed as $dm^3\,min^{-1}$) is calculated as:

tidal volume × breathing rate

A well-trained athlete can achieve adequate ventilation by increasing the tidal volume with only a small increase in the rate of breathing.

Successful gaseous exchange relies on matching ventilation with blood flow. The brain adjusts the ventilation rate and the flow of deoxygenated blood through the pulmonary artery according to need. It does this by monitoring the carbon dioxide concentration of the blood. If this increases, breathing becomes faster and deeper so that more air ventilates the gaseous exchange surface.

Pulse rate

When the heart contracts, a surge of blood flows into the aorta and the pulmonary arteries under pressure. The volume of blood pumped out from each ventricle during each contraction is the **stroke volume**. The total volume pumped out per minute is the **cardiac output**. The surge of blood distends arteries, which contain elastic tissue. The stretch and subsequent recoil of the aorta and the arteries travels as a wave along all the arteries. This is the **pulse**. The **pulse rate** is identical to the heart rate. The pulse is usually taken at the wrist where the radial artery passes over a bone, or over the carotid artery in the neck. The pulse is counted for thirty seconds and the result doubled to obtain the resting pulse rate in beats per minute.

The resting pulse rate is an indication of fitness. At rest, the cardiac output is about $5\,dm^3$ of blood every minute. This can be achieved by having a large stroke volume with a low resting pulse rate, or a small stroke volume with a higher pulse rate. The heart uses less energy when pumping slowly than when pumping at a higher rate. Also if it beats slowly at rest, its rate does not have to increase too much during exercise. People who are physically fit often have a low resting pulse; their pulse rates return to normal quickly after exercise. Endurance athletes in particular usually have large hearts with low pulse rates.

Pulse rate	Level of fitness
less than 50	outstanding
50–59	excellent
60–69	good
70–79	fair
80 and over	poor

● **Table 3.2** Resting pulse rates and levels of fitness

The normal range of resting pulse rates is 60 to 100 beats per minute (*table 3.2*). The average in fit young adults is about 70, and falls with age. The pulse rate is higher during and after exercise, and also after eating or smoking. It is at its lowest when people are asleep.

Box 3A Measuring lung volumes

Ventilation brings about changes in lung volume, and these changes can be measured by a **spirometer**. In the spirometer shown in *figure 3.6* a person breathes from a tube connected to an oxygen-containing chamber that floats on a tank of water. The chamber falls during inhalation and rises during exhalation. A canister of soda lime absorbs all the carbon dioxide in the exhaled air. The chamber does not rise to the same height with each breath because oxygen is absorbed in the lungs. The movements of the chamber are recorded on a kymograph trace (*figure 3.7*).

Two measures can be obtained from the trace: tidal volume and vital capacity.

■ **Tidal volume** is the volume of air breathed in and then breathed out during a single breath. The tidal volume at rest is about $0.5\,dm^3$ ($500\,cm^3$).

■ **Vital capacity** is the maximum volume of air that can be breathed in and then breathed out of the lungs by movement of the diaphragm and ribs. In young men the average is about $4.6\,dm^3$; in young women it is about $3.1\,dm^3$. In elite athletes the figures may be as much as $6.0\,dm^3$ for men and $4.5\,dm^3$ for women.

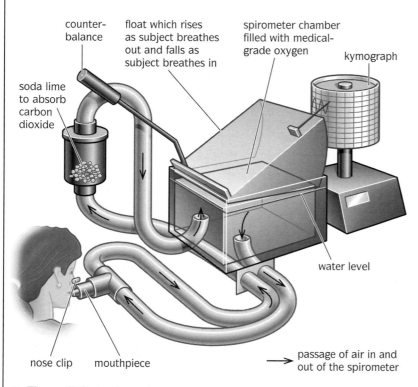

counter-balance

float which rises as subject breathes out and falls as subject breathes in

spirometer chamber filled with medical-grade oxygen

kymograph

soda lime to absorb carbon dioxide

water level

nose clip   mouthpiece

passage of air in and out of the spirometer

● *Figure 3.6* A spirometer.

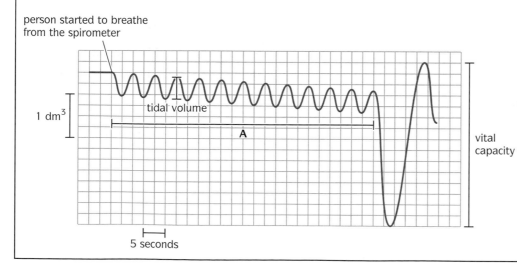

person started to breathe from the spirometer

1 dm³

tidal volume

A

5 seconds

vital capacity

● *Figure 3.7* A kymograph trace of a 17-year-old male with a mass of 70 kg who breathed normally, took a deep breath and breathed out as much as possible. The drum revolves at a speed of $2.5\,mm\,s^{-1}$.

Blood pressure

The left ventricle contracts to force blood out under pressure. The maximum arterial pressure during this active stroke is the **systolic pressure** and this is the pressure at which blood leaves the heart through the aorta. As the heart relaxes, the pressure in the left ventricle falls, so that the high pressure in the aorta closes the semilunar valve. Elastic recoil of the aorta and the main arteries provides a head of pressure to maintain a steady flow of blood in the arteries towards the capillaries.

The minimum pressure in the arteries is the **diastolic pressure**. The value of the diastolic pressure reflects the resistance of the small arteries and capillaries to blood flow and therefore the load against which the heart must work. If the resistance is high, so is the diastolic pressure. This can be the result of the blood vessels not stretching very well because of atherosclerosis or arteriosclerosis (see page 5).

Blood pressures are determined using a **sphygmomanometer** *(box 3B)*; it is conventional to give the values in millimetres of mercury (mm Hg). Typical blood pressure are:

■ systolic – 120 mm Hg (equivalent to 15.8 kPa);
■ diastolic – 80 mm Hg (equivalent to 10.5 kPa).

This is often written as 120/80 (120 over 80). Both pressures rise and fall during the day. Blood pressures change with age: for a young adult they may be 110/75, but by age 60 years they could be 130/90.

SAQ 3.4

Suggest some factors that might affect blood pressure during the day.

SAQ 3.5

Explain why blood pressure increases with age.

Hypertension

Blood pressure is a measure of how hard the heart is working to pump blood around the body. Systolic pressure may rise during exercise to 200 mm Hg; diastolic pressure rarely changes very much in healthy people, even during strenuous exercise. If systolic and diastolic blood pressures are high at rest, this indicates that the heart is working hard at pumping blood. This condition is known as **hypertension**.

Population surveys show that there is a normal distribution of blood pressure (a bell-shaped curve). There is no sharp distinction between 'normal' and

---

Box 3B Measuring blood pressure

The traditional way to measure blood pressure is with a mercury sphygmomanometer *(figure 3.8)*. The rubber cuff of the sphygmomanometer is inflated to give a pressure of 200 mm Hg. This stops the flow of blood into the brachial artery. A stethoscope is placed over the artery and the cuff deflated gradually. The systolic pressure is the pressure when the heart beat is first heard as a soft tapping sound. The cuff is deflated further until the sounds disappear. The diastolic pressure is the pressure when sounds can no longer be heard. Dual blood pressure and pulse rate monitors with digital displays are much easier for untrained people to use.

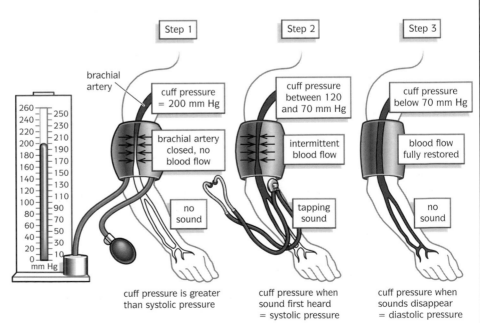

● **Figure 3.8** The use of a mercury sphygmomanometer to measure blood pressure.

Category	*Blood pressure/mm Hg*	
	systolic	*diastolic*
below normal	< 100	< 60
normal	100–139	60–89
borderline	140–159	90–94
hypertension	> 159	> 94

● **Table 3.3** The World Health Organisation classification of adult blood pressures

high blood pressure. However, the risks of cardio-vascular diseases such as stroke and coronary heart disease increase considerably with blood pressures in excess of 140/90. The World Health Organisation classifies the resting blood pressures of adults into four groups (table 3.3). Hypertension is taken as a blood pressure higher than 160/95. In Britain 15–20% of adults may be hypertensive.

The causes of high blood pressure are generally unknown. In the short term it occurs because of contraction of smooth muscle in the walls of small arteries and arterioles. This may happen because of an increase in the concentration of the hormone noradrenaline in the blood, which stimulates arterioles to contract. This increases the resistance of the blood vessels and so the heart works harder to force blood through the circulatory system. However, this does not explain long-term hypertension.

Long-term hypertension imposes a strain on the cardiovascular system and if not corrected can lead to heart failure, which occurs when heart muscles weaken and are unable to pump properly. Hypertension is known as the 'silent killer' as there are often no prior symptoms to give a warning of impending heart failure, heart attack (p. 44) or stroke. In 90% of cases the causes of hypertension are unknown, but the condition is closely linked to:

■ moderate to excessive alcohol intake (the consumption of 80 g of alcohol a week – equivalent to four pints of beer – often increases blood pressure);
■ smoking;
■ obesity;

■ salt in the diet;
■ genetic factors (people who have close relatives who are hypertensive may also be at risk even if they are not in a high risk category in terms of the other factors such as smoking or obesity).

Energy and exercise

During exercise, muscles use large quantities of energy. There are four sources of energy available to muscles (figure 3.9):

1 a small amount of **ATP** and **creatine phosphate (CP)** in muscle cells (CP is a reserve store of energy that is used to regenerate ATP);
2 **glycogen** stored in muscle cells;
3 **fatty acids** supplied from adipose tissue in muscles and elsewhere;
4 **glucose** in the blood, 'topped up' by glucose released from stores of glycogen in the liver.

During exercise the small store of ATP is soon exhausted, although it provides enough energy for 'explosive' events such as shot put. If exercise continues for longer than a few seconds, ATP is resynthesised from CP. Stores of ATP and CP last for a few seconds to provide energy for a brief sprint during a game of soccer or hockey. Anaerobic respiration of glycogen provides energy for exercise that takes longer than a few seconds.

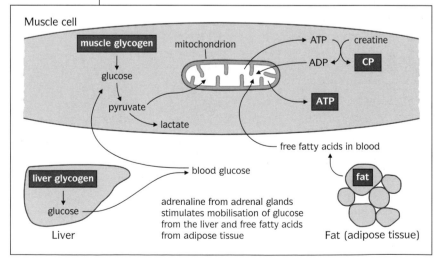

● **Figure 3.9** The sources of energy available to muscles. Creatine is phosphorylated by ATP when the muscle is at rest. During exercise creatine phosphate (CP) is used to phosphorylate ADP to give ATP without having to use respiration. CP only provides enough energy for short bursts of activity.

Respiration has to be anaerobic because the supply of oxygen in the blood cannot meet the demands of the muscles when exercise begins.

Oxygen for respiration in muscles comes from two sources:

1 oxyhaemoglobin in the blood;
2 oxymyoglobin stored in muscle.

Myoglobin is a protein similar to haemoglobin that combines with oxygen. It holds it more strongly, however, until there is a very low concentration of oxygen in the muscles.

At rest a small quantity of blood flows through the muscles as only one in 30 or 40 of the capillaries is open; only about 20% of the heart's output flows through these capillaries. During exercise this volume increases as blood is diverted away from the gut and skin to the muscles. Arterioles in muscles dilate and capillary flow increases. This adjustment takes a while to be effective. Similarly, the heart and lungs take time to adjust to the increased demand for oxygen, so the supply of oxygen to muscles at the beginning of exercise is insufficient for the rate of aerobic respiration needed to meet the demand for energy. The lag in oxygen uptake at the beginning of exercise is the **oxygen deficit**.

On your marks ...

Imagine you are about to take part in an athletic event – a run, swim or cycle race. Before starting, your body anticipates the increase in energy demand that will happen as soon as you begin. The hormone **adrenaline** flows into the blood causing the heart rate and ventilation rate to increase. Arterioles in the skin and gut constrict; those in the muscles dilate. Glucose is mobilised from the liver, fat is mobilised from adipose tissue. The race begins. The demand for energy increases very steeply. Muscles use the small quantity of

ATP and change it into ADP. ATP is resynthesised from CP, which lasts for a few seconds. An increase in the ratio of ADP to ATP stimulates glycolysis so that glycogen is broken down to glucose, which is oxidised to pyruvate. Some pyruvate is respired in mitochondria using oxygen from oxymyoglobin and that supplied by the blood. The limited supply of oxygen forces the muscles to gain most of their energy from anaerobic respiration. Pyruvate is converted into **lactate**, which diffuses into the blood.

If the race lasts for a very short time, most of the energy will be provided by the immediate energy system: there is enough ATP and CP for about six to eight seconds of exercise. If exercise continues for longer than this, the energy is supplied by the short-term or anaerobic energy system which releases lactate. This system produces ATP and CP at a rapid rate to allow strenuous exercise to continue beyond a few seconds. For example, after three minutes of hard cycling the total quantity of lactate in the blood may be about 7 g.

Strenuous exercise in explosive events is powered anaerobically by the immediate and

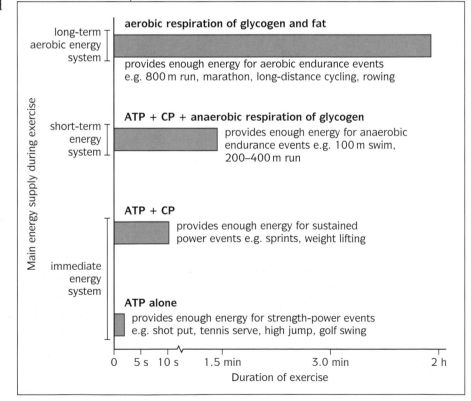

● *Figure 3.10* The three energy systems that supply energy for exercise: immediate, short-term and long-term.

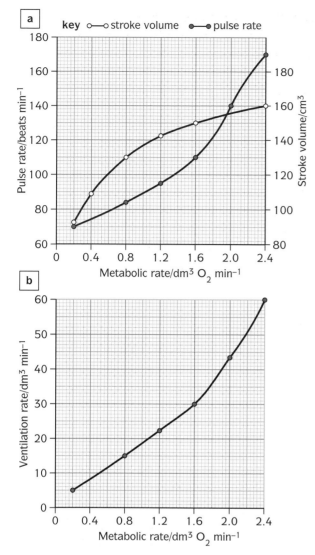

● *Figure 3.11* Increases in **a** pulse rate and stroke volume, and **b** ventilation rate during exercise.

short-term energy systems. This 'buys time' until the long-term aerobic energy system can operate efficiently. The three energy systems used in exercise are shown in *figure 3.10*.

SAQ 3.6

a Use *figure 3.11* to calculate the total cardiac output at the following metabolic rates: $0.8\,dm^3\ O_2\ min^{-1}$; $1.6\,dm^3\ O_2\ min^{-1}$; $2.4\,dm^3\ O_2\ min^{-1}$.

b Describe the adjustments that are made in the cardio-vascular and gas exchange systems at the beginning of exercise.

Nicotinamide adenine dinucleotide (**NAD**) is a coenzyme used in respiration. Muscle cells only have a small quantity of NAD, so it must be continually recycled if glycolysis is to continue, as it is needed for the oxidation of triose phosphate. The recycling happens when pyruvate is reduced to lactate; NAD is converted back into its oxidised form allowing anaerobic respiration to continue transferring energy from glycogen to ATP.

The flow of lactate and carbon dioxide into the tissue fluid stimulates the arterioles to dilate and increases the blood flow in muscles. An increase in the carbon dioxide concentration in the blood stim-ulates an increase in the ventilation rate. Adrenaline stimulates bronchioles to dilate so that the resistance to air flow in the lungs decreases. These adjustments improve the supply of oxygen to muscles. The rate of aerobic respiration can now increase and the long-term energy supply system takes over.

As blood flows through muscle capillaries the dissociation of oxyhaemoglobin to release oxygen is increased by:

■ low oxygen concentration in muscle tissue;
■ high carbon dioxide concentration;
■ low pH (due to accumulation of lactate);
■ high temperature.

SAQ 3.7

Explain why the pH of the blood decreases from its resting value to 7.4 to 7.0 during exercise.

The long-term energy system uses a mixture of blood glucose, glycogen and fat. Adrenaline stimu-lates the breakdown of fat in adipose tissue so that free fatty acids are transported in the plasma to muscles. The average 70 kg male has enough stored fat to provide energy for a 3000 mile walk.

Very little lactate accumulates if sufficient oxygen is supplied by the cardiovascular system to support the aerobic respiration required to power the muscles. However, the lactate that accumulates in the first few minutes of exercise needs to be removed. When exercise is very intense and the energy demand is greater than can be supported by the long-term system, then it is likely that fatigue will set in and exercise will cease. Lactate is an early warning device. As it accumulates in muscle cells, pH decreases and enzymes become less efficient.

Less energy is released, fatigue sets in and exercise stops. Lactate is not excreted: it is a rich source of energy and is recycled in the liver by means of the Cori cycle (*figure 3.12*).

The reduced NAD, formed when lactate is converted to pyruvate in the liver, is oxidised in mitochondria with the formation of ATP. In this way, lactate, in being a temporary store of hydrogen, is used to regenerate ATP that could not be formed in muscle because of the shortage of oxygen.

After exercise, ventilation rates fall steeply, but they do not return to pre-exercise levels for some time (*figure 3.13*). This is because extra oxygen is required for:

■ respiring lactate in the liver (*figure 3.12*);
■ reoxygenating myoglobin in muscles;
■ reoxygenating haemoglobin in the blood;
■ resynthesising ATP and CP in muscle cells;
■ supporting a high metabolic rate, as all organs are operating at above resting levels.

During the recovery period the uptake of oxygen remains high to restore oxygen levels in the body. This post-exercise oxygen uptake is sometimes called the **oxygen debt**.

SAQ 3.8

Explain why there is a lag in oxygen uptake at the beginning of exercise.

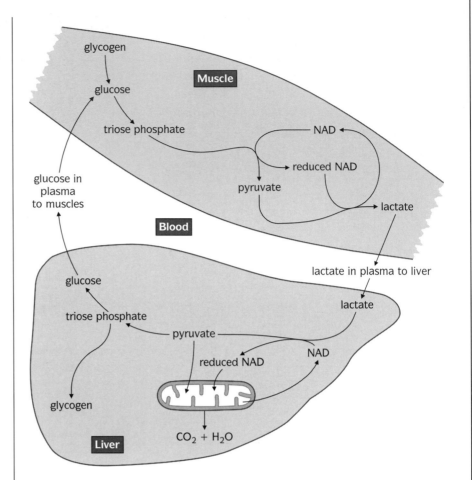

● *Figure 3.12* The Cori cycle. Lactate is produced in muscle cells. This allows glycolysis to continue as its production involves the resynthesis of NAD. Lactate is a temporary store of hydrogen for later use in oxidative phosphorylation in the liver where it is recycled to glucose and glycogen.

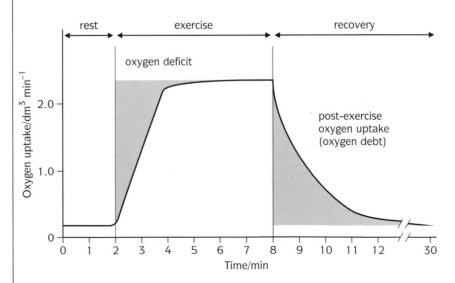

● *Figure 3.13* Oxygen uptake before, during and after strenuous exercise. The post-exercise oxygen uptake (oxygen debt) is that amount over and above the resting uptake (unshaded area) during recovery.

During endurance events, such as middle to long distance running, cycling and swimming, oxygen demand during exercise must equal oxygen uptake. An athlete's success depends upon the efficiency with which the gas exchange and cardiovascular systems can supply oxygen to the muscles to sustain high rates of aerobic respiration. During endurance events athletes respire a mixture of glycogen (stored in muscles), blood glucose and fatty acids. When the blood glucose is low and glycogen exhausted, these athletes 'hit the wall'. Maximum power declines when carbohydrate stores are low, as they provide the Krebs cycle intermediates required to respire fat. All athletes have more than enough fat and can supply suffi-cient oxygen for long-term exercise. It is the store of carbohydrate which is the limiting factor. This explains why marathon runners take glucose drinks at intervals. They also increase the glycogen content of their muscles by eating food rich in carbohydrates, such as pasta, shortly after a training session. The carbohydrate in the diet is converted into muscle glycogen to replenish the stores exhausted during training.

Aerobic fitness

If you exercise regularly, the body adapts so that it can carry out exercise more efficiently. **Aerobic exercise** is that which uses the gaseous exchange and cardiovascular systems: it includes everything from brisk walking to cycling, swimming and marathon running. This type of exercise improves the capacity of the circulation to deliver blood and it develops the metabolic machinery in muscles to consume oxygen and supply energy efficiently. With training, the heart and lungs become more efficient and the muscles produce greater quantities of the enzymes used in respiration.

A measure of a person's aerobic fitness is the maximum rate at which the body can absorb and utilise oxygen. This is known as $\dot{V}_{O_2}$ max. It is measured by recording a person's oxygen uptake with a gas analyser while they exercise on a tread-mill (*figure 3.14*). By increasing the speed and gradient of the treadmill, the intensity of exercise

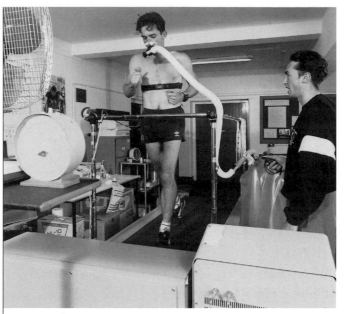

● *Figure 3.14* An athlete running on a treadmill while various physiological measurements of his heart and lungs are taken.

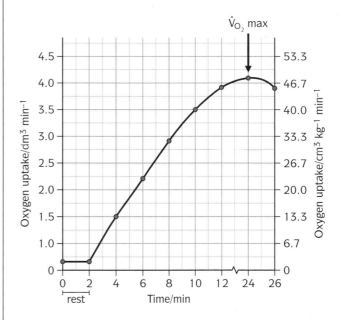

speed/ km h⁻¹	0	0	4.8	8.0	11.2	11.2	11.2	11.2	11.2
treadmill grade/%	0	0	0	5.5	7.5	9.5	11.5	13.5	15.5
time/min	0–2	2–4	4–6	6–8	8–10	10–12	12–24	24–26	26–28

● *Figure 3.15* Finding the $\dot{V}_{O_2}$ max. It is often expressed as the volume of O_2 used per kilogram body mass per minute. The table provides the speed, treadmill grade (slope) and duration values for each record plotted.

is increased. As the treadmill becomes faster and steeper, the person has to use more energy and the rate of aerobic respiration increases. Oxygen uptake continues to rise until it reaches a plateau (*figure 3.15*) or the person stops from exhaustion.

SAQ 3.9

a Suggest the factors that influence the $\dot{V}_{O_2}$ max.

b Suggest what happens when you exercise beyond your $\dot{V}_{O_2}$ max.

At your $\dot{V}_{O_2}$ max. your heart rate is near its maximum. (To calculate your maximum heart rate deduct your age from 220.) There is a strong correlation between pulse rate and $\dot{V}_{O_2}$ max. for different people. Taking the pulse rate during or immediately after exercise, or using the 'step test', are much simpler methods of assessing levels of aerobic fitness than the method shown in *figure 3.14*.

There are many benefits of exercise (*box 3C*). To improve aerobic fitness it is recommended that you work at 70% of your maximum heart rate for at least twenty minutes three times a week. This level of intensity represents about 50–55% of $\dot{V}_{O_2}$ max., which is considered to be the threshold for aerobic improvement. More intense exercise can be more effective, but no extra improvement is achieved by exercising for more than four or five times a week. Exercising below the threshold is equally effective if the duration is correspondingly longer. As fitness improves during training, the intensity of exercise must increase to maintain the desired training heart rate as cardiac output increases. Even mild exercise can be beneficial. The US Public Health Service guidelines recommend a half-hour walk every day. This uses about 650 kJ and confers some protection against heart disease.

Box 3C The benefits of exercise

Cardiovascular fitness
- fall in resting heart rate (may be by as much as 20 beats min^{-1})
- increase in stroke volume
- increase in cardiac output
- increase in heart size, slight thickening of left ventricle wall
- decrease in resting systolic and diastolic pressures
- improved supply of blood to muscles during exercise
- more powerful heart beat

Respiratory fitness
- increase in tidal volume
- increase in vital capacity
- steady rate of oxygen uptake during exercise reached more quickly

Muscles
- increase in muscle size
- increase in capillary density, so shorter diffusion distance for oxygen from blood to muscle cells
- increase in size of muscle fibres
- increase in number and size of mitochondria
- more glycogen and fat stored in muscles
- increase in quantities of respiratory enzymes
- enhanced ability to transfer energy to ATP from fatty acids
- increase in myoglobin stored in muscles

Health benefits
- decrease in blood pressure for people with hypertension
- enhanced utilisation of fat (increase in lipase in adipose tissue)
- loss in weight
- improved resistance to infection
- reduced risk of osteoporosis in females
- reduced risk of CHD and stroke
- decrease in plasma cholesterol concentration
- slowing down of atherosclerosis
- improvement in balance, coordination, strength and flexibility
- strengthening of ligaments, tendons and bones
- reduced chance of lower back pain
- psychological benefits

SUMMARY

■ Air passes down the trachea and through a branching system of airways in the lungs to reach the alveoli. The airways are lined by a ciliated epithelium with mucus-secreting goblet cells. The epithelium protects the alveoli by moving a carpet of mucus towards the throat. The alveoli are the site of gaseous exchange.

■ A spirometer measures the tidal volume and vital capacity of the lungs. Tidal volume is the volume of air breathed in and then out. At rest it is about $0.5 \, dm^3$. Vital capacity is the maximum volume of air that can be breathed out after fully inflating the lungs.

■ The pulse rate is identical to the heart rate. Resting pulse rate is used as a measurement of aerobic fitness since a low rate is associated with a large volume of blood expelled by the heart with each beat.

■ Blood in the arteries is under pressure. When the heart contracts, this pressure rises. The maximum pressure which corresponds to the emptying of the left ventricle is the systolic pressure. The minimum pressure in the arteries occurs when the left ventricle is relaxed and filling with blood. This is the diastolic pressure.

■ Hypertension is high blood pressure. The causes of this are unknown, but appear to be related to genetic factors, a diet rich in salt, consumption of alcohol and obesity. High blood pressure is a contributory factor to coronary heart disease.

■ The lungs and heart make adjustments during exercise to deliver oxygen to respiring tissues. The ventilation rate (tidal volume × rate of breathing) and cardiac output (stroke volume × heart rate) both increase during exercise.

■ Aerobic exercise is any form of exercise that uses the heart and lungs to provide oxygen for aerobic respiration in muscles. Explosive events, such as weight lifting, do not require energy from aerobic respiration during exercise; all the energy is provided by anaerobic respiration. Aerobic exercise includes everything from walking to endurance events such as long-distance cycling, running and swimming.

■ $\dot{V}_{O_2}$ max. is a measure of aerobic fitness, and is found by measuring oxygen uptake or by taking the recovery pulse rate. A low pulse rate during recovery and at rest indicates a high level of aerobic fitness.

Questions

1 a Describe how the structure of the lungs is adapted to absorb oxygen.
   b Describe how the lung surfaces are protected from damage.

2 Describe how measurements of lung volumes are made.

3 Explain the term *aerobic exercise* and describe how aerobic fitness can be assessed.

4 Describe the adjustments made in the body at the beginning of strenuous exercise.

5 Explain the difference in the provision of energy for an explosive event, such as a sprint, and an endurance event, such as long distance cycling.

6 Discuss the importance of exercise in maintaining good health.

7 Measure the tidal volume and vital capacity from the trace in *figure 3.7*.

8 For the part of the trace labelled A in *figure 3.7*, calculate:
   a the rate of breathing in breaths per minute;
   b the ventilation rate (tidal volume × breathing rate);
   c the volume of oxygen absorbed per minute.

9 a At rest people use 1dm3 of oxygen for every 21.2kJ of energy released in respiration. This is a measurement of basal metabolic rate (BMR). Use your answer to 8c to calculate the BMR in kJ per day for the person whose trace is shown in *figure 3.7*.
   b The BMR for a 17-year-old male is about 7300kJ per day. Suggest reasons for the differences between this figure and the one you have calculated in a.

Chapter four

Smoking and disease

By the end of this chapter you should be able to:

1 describe the effects of tar and carcinogens in tobacco smoke on the gaseous exchange system;

2 describe the symptoms of chronic obstructive pulmonary disease (chronic bronchitis and emphysema) and lung cancer;

3 evaluate the epidemiological and experimental evidence linking cigarette smoking to disease and early death;

4 describe the effects of nicotine and carbon monoxide in tobacco smoke on the cardiovascular system with reference to atherosclerosis, coronary heart disease and strokes;

5 discuss the reasons for the global distribution of coronary heart disease;

6 discuss the difficulty in achieving a balance between prevention and cure with reference to coronary heart disease and heart transplant surgery.

Lung diseases

Healthy people breathe with little conscious effort; for people with lung diseases every breath may be a struggle. The lungs are susceptible to disease as they have such a large surface area exposed to the air. They are constantly exposed to moving streams of air carrying noxious chemicals and, because the filtering system in the airways is not always efficient, very small particles (< 2 µm in diameter) often reach the alveoli and stay there. Traffic exhaust and tobacco smoke contain such particles. It is a serious risk to the health of people who live or work in dusty or smoky environments.

The air that flows down the trachea with each breath fills the huge volume of tiny airways. The small particles settle out easily because the air flow in the depths of the lungs is very slow. They make the lungs much more susceptible to airborne infections such as influenza and pneumonia. In addition, **allergens** (substances that cause allergies), such as pollen and the faeces of house dust mites,

trigger a defence mechanism in the cells lining the airways. If this is very bad it may cause an asthmatic attack which causes the smooth muscles in the airways to contract, obstructing the flow of air and making breathing difficult. The body's defence mechanisms may react with the production of more mucus and the collection of white blood cells in the airways. This can block the airways and cause severe bouts of coughing, which can damage the alveoli. Continuous damage can lead to the replacement of the thin alveolar surface by scar tissue, so reducing the surface area for diffusion. This replacement also happens when particles of coal dust or asbestos regularly reach the alveoli.

Chronic (or long-term) **obstructive lung diseases** are now more common as a result of atmospheric pollution and smoking. After heart disease and strokes, lung diseases are the most common cause of illness and death in the UK. It is estimated that one in seven children in the UK suffers from asthma.

Tobacco smoke

In the 1950s the link between smoking and lung cancer was recognised. Smoking was later found to be a risk factor in heart disease.

Tobacco smoke is composed of 'mainstream smoke' from the filter or mouth end of a cigarette, and 'sidestream smoke' from the burning tip. Typically, about 85% of the smoke in a room is sidestream smoke. There are over 4000 different chemicals in cigarette smoke. Many of the toxic compounds are found in higher concentration in the sidestream smoke than in the mainstream smoke putting others, as well as the smoker, at risk of smoking-related diseases. Breathing in someone else's cigarette smoke is called **passive smoking**.

Three main components of cigarette smoke pose a threat to human health:

1 tar – a mixture of aromatic compounds;

2 carbon monoxide;

3 nicotine.

Tar is implicated in the development of chronic obstructive pulmonary disease and lung cancer.

Chronic obstructive pulmonary disease

Chronic obstructive pulmonary disease (COPD) is a progressively disabling disease. Sufferers experience difficulty in breathing because of the blockage of the small airways and destruction of alveoli. The gradual onset of breathlessness only becomes troublesome when about half of the lung is destroyed. Only in very rare circumstances is it reversible. If smoking is given up when still young, lung function can improve. In older people such improvement is not possible. As the blood is not so well oxygenated the blood pressure in the pulmonary artery increases. The right side of the heart enlarges and fluid accumulates in the body, especially in the legs.

The blockage of the airways is caused by chronic bronchitis. In long-term smokers, it is often accompanied by emphysema, which destroys the alveoli. Emphysema afflicts one in five of all smokers.

Chronic bronchitis

Tar in tobacco smoke inhibits the cleaning action of the lungs. It stimulates the goblet cells in the epithelium of the airways to secrete more mucus and also inhibits the sweeping action of the cilia. As a result mucus accumulates in the bronchioles and the smallest of these may be obstructed. As mucus is not moved, or at best is only moved slowly, dirt, bacteria and viruses collect and cause 'smoker's cough'. The changes to the linings of the airways can be summarised as follows:

- mucus glands in the trachea and bronchi enlarge;
- mucus glands and goblet cells produce much more mucus;
- cilia are destroyed;
- epithelia are replaced by scar tissue;
- smooth muscle becomes thicker;
- airways are blocked by mucus.

These changes constitute chronic bronchitis. Sufferers have a severe cough, producing large quantities of phlegm, which is a mixture of mucus, bacteria and some white cells. Bronchitis usually contributes to the development of emphysema.

Emphysema

As the lung's protective system is compromised by chronic bronchitis, infections become more common. This leads to inflammation in the lungs: more macrophages line the lungs and phagocytes join them from the blood. These phagocytes release the protein-digesting enzyme elastase to reach the surface of the alveoli. Elastase destroys elastin in the connective tissue so that the alveoli do not stretch and recoil when breathing in and out *(figure 4.1)*. Because of this, the bronchioles collapse during exhalation trapping air in the alveoli, which often burst. Large spaces appear where they have burst and this reduces the surface area for gaseous exchange. Cells in the alveoli release an elastase inhibitor (α_1 antitrypsin), but some smokers produce less of this than non-smokers, so there is little to reduce the effect of the phagocytes. These smokers are very susceptible to developing emphysema.

The loss of elastin makes it difficult to move air out of the lungs. Non-smokers can force out about $4\,dm^3$ of air after taking a deep breath; someone with emphysema may manage to force out only $1.3\,dm^3$ of air. The air remains in the lungs and is not refreshed during ventilation. Together with the reduced surface area for gaseous exchange, this means that many people with emphysema do not oxygenate their blood very well and have a very rapid breathing rate.

As lung function deteriorates, wheezing occurs and breathlessness becomes progressively worse. It may become so bad in some people that they cannot get out of bed. Towards the end most people with emphysema often need a continuous supply of oxygen through a face mask to stay alive. In *figure 4.2*, it is possible to compare diseased and relatively unaffected lung tissue.

SAQ 4.1

Summarise the changes that occur in the lungs of people with bronchitis and emphysema.

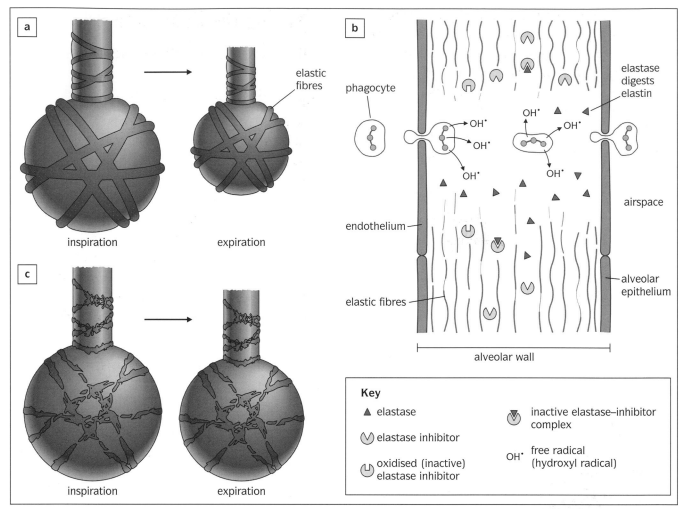

● **Figure 4.1** The development of emphysema. **a** Healthy alveoli partially deflate during expiration.
b Phagocytes from the blood make pathways through alveolar walls by digesting elastin. **c** As a result of
many years of this destruction the alveoli do not deflate very much.

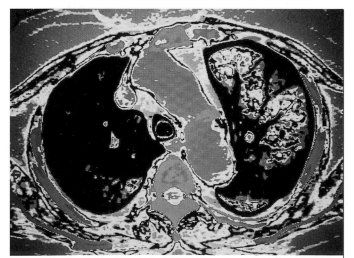

● **Figure 4.2** A computed tomography scan (CT scan) of
a horizontal section through the thorax. The lung on the
right is diseased with emphysema. The lung on the left
is relatively unaffected at the level of this scan.

Tar, carcinogens and lung cancer

Tar in tobacco smoke contains several substances
that have been identified as carcinogens. These
react, directly or via breakdown products, with
DNA in epithelial cells to produce mutations, which
are the first in a series of changes that lead to the
development of a malignant tumour *(figure 1.1)*.

As the cancer develops, it spreads through the
bronchial epithelium and enters the lymphoid tissues
in the lung (see page 68). Metastasis may occur with
secondary cells breaking away from the tumour and
establishing themselves in organs such as the liver,
adrenal glands and brain. The most common
symptom of lung cancer is coughing up blood.

Lung cancer takes 20 to 30 years to develop.
Most of the growth of a tumour occurs before

there are any symptoms. It is rare for a cancer to be diagnosed before it reaches 1 cm in diameter. By that time it has already doubled in size 30 times from the moment of the malignant mutation.

Tumours in the lungs, such as that shown in *figure 4.3*, are located by one of three methods:

1 bronchoscopy, using an endoscope to allow a direct view of the lining of the bronchi;
2 chest X-ray;
3 CT scan (similar to that shown in *figure 4.2*).

By the time most lung cancers are discovered they are well advanced and the only hope is to remove them by surgery. If the cancer is small and in one lung, then either a part, or all, of the lung is removed. However, metastasis has usually happened by the time of the diagnosis, so if there are secondary tumours then surgery will not cure the disease. Chemotherapy with anti-cancer drugs or radiotherapy with X-rays (or other form of radiation) will be used.

● *Figure 4.3* A scanning electron micrograph of a bronchial carcinoma – a cancer in a bronchus. Cancers often develop at the base of the trachea where it divides into the bronchi as this is where most of the tar is deposited. The disorganised malignant tumour cells at the bottom right are invading the normal tissue of the ciliated epithelium. (× 200).

Proving the links between smoking and lung disease

Epidemiological evidence

The link between smoking and lung cancer was first made in the 1950s. Tobacco had been available in Europe since the 16th century, but it was mostly smoked in pipes or as cigars. Cigarettes were manufactured from the end of the 19th century and only became fashionable amongst men during the First World War. Women did not begin smoking in large numbers until the 1940s. Doctors started noticing cases of lung cancer from the 1930s onwards, and then from the 1950s there was an epidemic *(figure 4.4)*. Epidemiologists

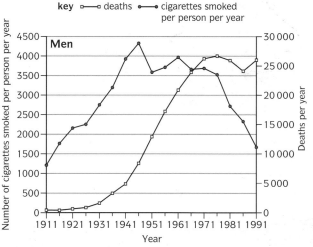

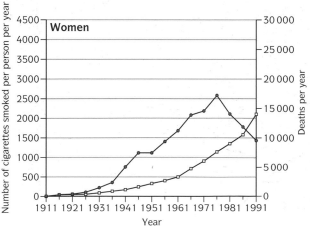

● *Figure 4.4* The smoking epidemic: the correlation between the consumption of cigarettes and deaths from lung cancer in the UK from 1911 to 1991.

Number of cigarettes smoked per day	Annual death rate per 100 000 men
0	10
1–14	78
15–24	127
> 25	251

Note that these are deaths from all causes not just lung cancer.

● **Table 4.1** Results of a study carried out on male doctors in Britain, showing that the risk of early death increases with the number of cigarettes smoked per day

discovered a correlation between lung cancer and cigarette smoking. In 1912 there were 374 cases of lung cancer; now there are over 35 000 deaths each year in the UK from the disease. Epidemiological data showing the link between smoking and lung diseases including cancer are summarised in box 4A. *Table 4.1* shows the correlation between the number of cigarettes smoked per day and the risk of early death.

SAQ 4.2

Summarise the trends shown in *figure 4.4*.

Conclusions drawn from epidemiological data about the risks of developing lung cancer could be criticised because they only show that there is an *association* between the two, not a causal link between them. There may be another common factor which is the causative one. For example, exposure to atmospheric pollutants such as sulphur

dioxide could be a cause. However, epidemiological studies have ruled out these other factors – comparably close correlations with them cannot be found. With smoking, on the other hand, it is possible to show a direct link with lung cancer because smoking is the common factor in almost all cases. Reports by the Royal College of Physicians published in 1962, 1971, 1977, 1983 and 1992 reviewed the epidemiological evidence for the link.

Experimental evidence

Experimental evidence shows a direct causative link between smoking and lung cancer. There are two lines of evidence.

1 Tumours similar to those found in humans develop in animals exposed to cigarette smoke.
2 Carcinogens have been identified in tar.

In the 1960s experimental animals were used to investigate the effect of cigarette smoke on the lungs (*figure 4.5*). In one study 48 dogs were divided into two groups. One group was made to smoke filter-tipped cigarettes and did not develop cancer. The other group smoked plain (unfiltered) cigarettes and developed abnormalities similar to those in human lung cancer patients. The animals also showed changes similar to those caused by COPD. The fact that the group smoking filter-tipped cigarettes remained healthy does not show that the filters remove all the carcinogens from

---

Box 4A The smoking epidemic.
Epidemiological evidence links smoking with lung diseases and early death.

General
■ Up to 50% of smokers may die of smoking-related diseases.
■ Smokers are three times more likely to die in middle age than non-smokers.

Chronic obstructive pulmonary disease
■ COPD is very rare in non-smokers.
■ 90% of deaths from COPD are attributed to smoking.
■ 98% of people with emphysema are smokers.
■ 20% of smokers suffer from emphysema.
■ Deaths from pneumonia and influenza are twice as high among smokers.

Lung cancer
■ The risk of developing lung cancer increases if smokers inhale; start young; increase the number of cigarettes smoked per day; use high tar cigarettes; smoke for a long time (smoking one packet of cigarettes per day for forty years is eight times more hazardous than smoking two packets for twenty years).
■ The risk of developing lung cancer starts to decrease as soon as smoking is stopped, but it takes ten or more years to return to the same risk as a non-smoker.
■ Smokers are 18 times more likely to develop lung cancer than non-smokers.
■ One-third of all cancer deaths are a direct result of cigarette smoking.
■ 25% of smokers die of lung cancer.

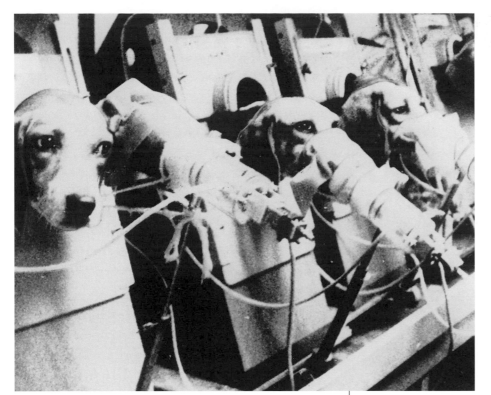

● *Figure 4.5* Beagles used in experiments in the 1960s to investigate the link between smoking and lung cancer. When the results were published they convinced many smokers to change to low tar, filter-tipped brands.

smoke. In fact some of the dogs developed pre-cancerous changes in the cells lining their airways.

Smoking machines, which copy the inhaling pattern of smokers, extract the chemicals contained in smoke. Chemical analysis of the black, oily liquid that accumulates in these machines shows that tar contains a variety of carcinogens and co-carcinogens. The latter are compounds which increase the likelihood that carcinogens will cause mutations in DNA. The most potent carcinogen is benzpyrene. When carcinogens from tar are painted onto the skin of mice, cancerous growths develop. Experiments like this not only confirm the link between smoking and lung cancer, they also help to show how tumours develop in the lungs.

The connection between cigarette smoking and lung cancer is irrefutable. The mechanisms by which carcinogens cause mutations and the factors that influence the growth of cancers are still being investigated. As the popularity of smoking decreases in developed countries, the smoking epidemic is spreading to the developing world, which, it is predicted, will see a rise in smoking-related diseases in the 21st century.

SAQ 4.3

Summarise the effects of tobacco smoke on the gaseous exchange system.

SAQ 4.4

It is estimated that smoking is responsible for 90% of all deaths from lung cancer, 76% of deaths from COPD and 16% of deaths from stroke and CHD. Use the data in *table 4.2* to calculate:

a the number of deaths in 1993 in (i) men and (ii) women that were attributable to smoking;

b the percentage of deaths of men and women that were attributable to smoking.

Disease	Men	Percentage of total deaths	Women	Percentage of total deaths	Total
lung cancer	24 963	7.87	12 757	3.75	37 720
COPD	18 826	5.93	11 848	3.48	30 674
stroke	26 310	8.29	44 976	13.21	71 286
CHD	90 774	28.62	76 831	22.57	167 605
all causes of death	317 194	100.00	340 373	100.00	657 567

● *Table 4.2* Deaths from lung cancer, COPD, stroke and CHD for all ages in the UK in 1993

Coronary heart disease

Degenerative diseases of the cardiovascular system (see page 5) killed an estimated 10 million people worldwide in 1993 (19% of the global total). The major cardiovascular diseases are coronary heart disease and stroke.

Coronary heart disease (CHD) is a disease of the arteries supplying blood to the heart muscles. It causes damage to, or malfunction of, the heart. Two coronary arteries branch from the aorta to supply all the muscles of the atria and ventricles.

SAQ. 4.5

Describe the functions of the coronary arteries.

The build up of fatty material in the lining of the coronary arteries (atherosclerosis) causes them to become narrow, therefore restricting the flow of blood. As a result the heart has to work harder to force blood through the arteries and this may cause blood pressure to rise. CHD develops, taking one or more of three forms.

1 *Angina pectoris*
   The main symptom of angina pectoris is severe chest pain brought on by exertion. The pain goes when resting. The pain is caused by a severe shortage of blood to the heart muscle, but there is no death of muscle tissue.
2 *Heart attack*
   This is also known as myocardial infarction. When a moderately large coronary artery is obstructed by a blood clot (thrombus) part of the heart muscle is starved of oxygen and dies. This causes sudden and severe chest pain. A heart attack may be fatal, but many people survive with immediate attention and treatment.
3 *Heart failure*
   The blockage of a main coronary artery leads to gradual damage of heart muscle with the result that the heart becomes weaker and fails to pump blood efficiently.

CHD was almost unknown before the 20th century and it is still mainly confined to developed countries. It is a disease associated with affluent countries, but as it is a degenerative disease it is likely that the incidence of CHD is high simply because of the increase in life span since 1900. High death rates from infectious diseases in earlier centuries obscured the degenerative changes that may have been occurring to people's coronary circulations. In other words, people did not die of CHD because they died of something else first.

Global distribution of coronary heart disease

Death rates from CHD differ markedly across the world: they are highest in northern Europe and lowest in Japan (*figure 4.6*).

Epidemiological data help to identify the risk factors involved in developing CHD. In the UK the incidence of CHD is highest:

■ in Scotland, Northern Ireland and the north and north-west of England;
■ among manual workers;
■ among certain ethnic groups (e.g. south Asians);
■ among men.

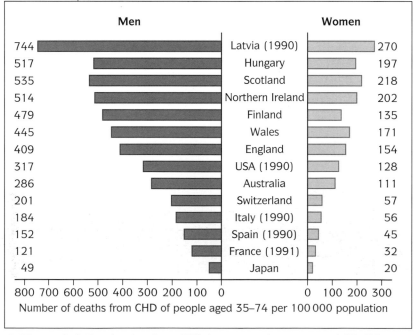

● **Figure 4.6** Death rates from CHD for men and women aged 35–74 per 100 000 population for selected countries. Unless stated otherwise the figures are for 1992.

CHD is a multifactorial disease. The risk factors shown in *table 4.3* have been identified in long-term epidemiological studies with large groups of people recording information about their ways of life, illnesses and causes of death. An American study of the population of a town in Massachusetts (the Framlingham study) and a study of civil servants in the UK (the Whitehall study) showed that:

- hypertension, high fat concentrations in the blood, cigarette smoking and diabetes were common factors among Americans who developed CHD;
- British civil servants who took regular exercise had half the incidence of CHD than their more sedentary colleagues.

To try to find the reasons for the global distribution of CHD, the World Health Organisation set up a multinational monitoring project (known as MONICA) in 1979. The project collects data on death rates from CHD and compares these with death rates from all causes. *Table 4.4* shows some results for two European countries with markedly different death rates for CHD. Rates tend to decline in a north-east to south-west direction across Europe. Finland and Spain are at opposite ends of this cline. Data were collected from North Karelia, a region in Finland which used to have the highest death rate from CHD in the world, and Catalonia in Spain.

Risk factor	Comments
age	risk increases with age, although CHD may begin in early life
sex	males are more at risk than women – before the menopause oestrogen protects women from developing CHD; after the menopause hormone replacement therapy (HRT) also gives protection
weight	being overweight or obese increases risk
diet	increased risk associated with high intake of animal (saturated) fat and the salt in manufactured foods
blood cholesterol	there is a direct relationship between concentration of cholesterol in the blood and risk of CHD; above $250\,\text{mg}\,100\,\text{cm}^{-3}$ is considered to be high and is likely to be due to high intake of saturated fat
high blood pressure	risk increases with increasing blood pressure
smoking	combines with other factors to multiply risks of CHD; promotes development of atherosclerosis
exercise	risk decreases as more exercise is taken
heredity	some families are at risk of high blood cholesterol concentrations
diabetes	diabetics are at a higher risk of developing CHD
alcohol	high intake raises blood pressure and increases risk of atherosclerosis; moderate intake may be protective
social class	heart disease is more prevalent among manual workers

● *Table 4.3* Risk factors associated with coronary heart disease

Country or region	Annual mortality/deaths per 100 000 population in age group 35–64 between 1984 and 1986							
	total number of deaths (all causes)		deaths from all cardiovascular diseases		deaths from CHD		deaths from stroke	
	men	women	men	women	men	women	men	women
Finland	894	314	427	103	317	52	57	32
North Karelia	1111	364	600	140	456	75	82	40
Spain	634	277	193	77	89	20	43	25
Catalonia	536	237	138	49	68	16	32	18

● *Table 4.4* Data on death rates collected from Finland and Spain as part of the of the WHO MONICA project

Risk factor		North Karelia percentage of		Catalonia percentage of	
		men	women	men	women
Total blood cholesterol/mg 100 cm^{-3}	normal (<200)	15	22	31	36
	borderline (200–250)	41	37	44	42
	high (250–300)	33	28	21	18
	very high (>300)	12	13	5	4
Systolic blood pressure/mm Hg	<140	43	48	84	84
	140–160	37	31	12	12
	>160	20	20	4	4
Diastolic blood pressure/mm Hg	< 90	56	67	91	93
	90–95	16	13	5	4
	>95	28	20	4	3
Body mass index	< 25 (acceptable and underweight)	32	40	34	31
	25–30 (overweight)	51	37	57	44
	>30 (obese)	17	23	9	24
Smoking	regular	29	8	47	7
	occasional	8	6	11	1
	ex-smoker	34	7	23	2
	non-smoker	29	79	20	90

● **Table 4.5** Risk factors for CHD in 35- to 64-year-olds in North Karelia and Catalonia (MONICA project)

The MONICA project also collects data on the risk factors associated with CHD. *Table 4.5* shows the results for North Karelia and Catalonia for five risk factors: total blood cholesterol concentration, systolic blood pressure, diastolic blood pressure, obesity (BMI – see page 22) and smoking. The populations of 35- to 64-year-olds were sampled for these risk factors and the results expressed as percentages of the male and female populations of this age group in the two regions.

SAQ 4.6

a Explain why results were collected for the 35–64 year age group and not for all age groups.

b Compare the populations of North Karelia and Catalonia in terms of the proportion of deaths due to (i) all cardiovascular diseases, (ii) CHD, and (iii) strokes.

c Suggest which members of the population of the two regions are most at risk of developing cardiovascular diseases.

SAQ 4.7

Review the epidemiological evidence given in *table 4.5* for the link between the five risk factors and deaths from cardiovascular diseases.

Many developed countries have taken steps to reduce the rate of heart disease. They encourage people to reduce their risk of developing the disease by taking more exercise, giving up smoking and decreasing the intake of animal fat. Death rates in these countries have fallen over the past 25 years, but whether this is as a result of these factors or not is uncertain. The USA and Australia in particular have seen significant reductions in death rates from CHD, possibly because people have taken heed of advice about reducing the risks.

The death rate from CHD in the UK is one of the highest in the world, especially in Scotland and Northern Ireland. In the UK, CHD accounts for a third of all deaths between the ages of 45 and 64. Although the death rate is decreasing in the UK partly as a result of better screening and treatment, it is still higher than in most other countries.

As CHD is a multifactorial disease, there is unlikely to be one simple reason for this. The results of the MONICA project suggest that diet, smoking, lack of exercise, obesity and high blood pressure are to blame. It is unlikely that genetic factors play a part. Death rates from CHD are low in both the Japanese and the Masai of East Africa. In both cases diet seems to be the main reason. When both groups abandon their traditional diets for typical Western ones, which are high in saturated fat, death rates from CHD increase.

Atherosclerosis

Atherosclerosis is the main cause of CHD. The inner layers of artery walls thicken with deposits of cholesterol, fibrous tissue, dead muscle cells and blood platelets. This substance is called **atheroma** and it forms plaques in the lining of the arteries, so making them less elastic.

The inside of a healthy artery is pale and smooth. Yellow fatty streaks start appearing in some people during childhood. These

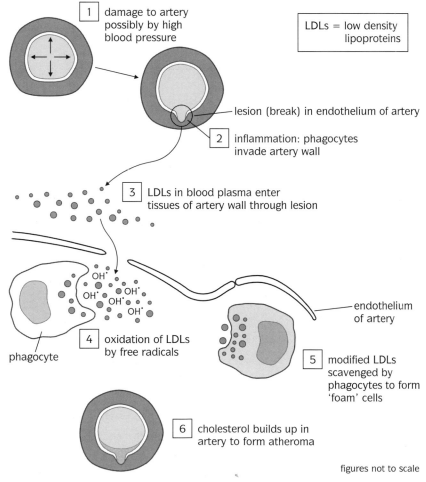

● *Figure 4.7* How damage to artery walls promotes the development of fatty plaques (atheromas).

start with damage to the lining, possibly caused by high blood pressure. The resulting breaks are invaded by phagocytes, which release growth factors that stimulate the growth of smooth muscle cells and the accumulation of cholesterol from the blood *(figure 4.7)*. Cholesterol is needed for the synthesis of vitamin D in the skin and hormones in the ovaries, testes and adrenal glands, and for making cell membranes in all tissues. It is not soluble in water and, like fats, is transported in the blood plasma by the following three different types of lipoprotein (see also *Transport, Regulation and Control* in this series, page 70).

1 Very low density lipoproteins (VLDLs), which transport fat to the tissues for storage.
2 Low density lipoproteins (LDLs), which are made from VLDLs in the tissues. They carry cholesterol from the liver (which makes cholesterol) to tissues that need it and those that do not (artery walls). LDLs are small enough to penetrate breaks in the artery lining and deposit cholesterol.
3 High density lipoproteins (HDLs), which remove cholesterol from tissues (including arteries) and transport it to the liver for excretion in the bile. This 'reverse cholesterol transport' carried out by HDLs protects the arteries from atherosclerosis.

Cholesterol deposited in the walls may be attacked by free radicals released by phagocytes. This damage may slow down the passage of LDLs back into the blood with the result that they deposit more cholesterol. When blood comes into contact with fatty and fibrous tissue, blood platelets stick to the roughened surface and release clotting factors called thromboxanes. In a healthy artery a balance exists between these and a prostaglandin. Both thromboxanes and prostaglandins are locally-acting signalling compounds derived from essential fatty acids (see page 17). The prostaglandin is released from endothelial cells lining the arteries to inhibit clotting, so that healthy vessels do not become blocked by blood clots. At the site of an atheroma, however, the balance between these two antagonistic compounds is upset and blood starts to clot.

Smoking, saturated fat and high blood pressure are risk factors for CHD. They probably promote atherosclerosis in the following ways.

Smoking:
- decreases the concentration of antioxidants in the blood (e.g. vitamins C and E), so increasing the damage done to artery walls by free radicals released by phagocytes;
- raises the number of platelets in the blood and makes them more sticky, stimulating the formation of blood clots;
- increases blood cholesterol and fat concentrations;
- causes constriction of coronary arteries;
- causes a rise in the ratio of VLDLs and LDLs to HDLs in the blood.

Saturated fat:
- decreases the number or activity of receptors for LDLs on liver cell membranes; (LDLs therefore remain in the circulation increasing the deposition of cholesterol on artery walls);
- increases blood cholesterol concentrations;
- causes a rise in the ratio of LDLs to HDLs.

High blood pressure:
- puts arteries under strain so that damage is more likely.

The narrowing of arteries caused by atherosclerosis leads to an increase in blood pressure, which weakens them further. Artery walls may stretch and balloon out to form an **aneurysm**. This may weaken the wall so much that it bursts. **Thrombosis** occurs when blood clots where atheromas roughen the lining of arteries. A clot, or **thrombus**, can interrupt the blood flow so that tissues are starved of oxygen and nutrients. An **embolism** occurs when a clot breaks away and lodges somewhere in the circulation.

Smoking is a major cause of **peripheral vascular disease** in which the supply of blood to the legs decreases. This can lead to gangrene and amputation. People who develop this disease and continue to ignore advice to give up smoking often have multiple amputations. There are over 2000 amputations a year carried out in England most of which are the result of peripheral vascular disease.

Smoking and coronary heart disease

The components of tobacco smoke that contribute to CHD are carbon monoxide and nicotine. The effects of these two compounds interact to increase the risk of developing a multifactorial disease such as CHD.

Carbon monoxide

Carbon monoxide is absorbed by the blood in the alveoli and competes with oxygen for haemoglobin. Haemoglobin has a greater affinity for carbon monoxide than it does for oxygen and forms the stable compound carboxyhaemoglobin. As haemoglobin is permanently bound to carbon monoxide this reduces the quantity of oxygen transported in the blood by as much as 5 to 10%. This increases the strain put on the cardiovascular system to deliver oxygen to tissues, such as heart muscle.

Nicotine

Nicotine is absorbed very readily by the blood and travels to the brain within a few seconds. It stimulates the sympathetic nervous system to reduce the diameter of the arterioles and to release adrenaline from the adrenal glands. This increases heart rate and blood pressure. There is a decrease in blood supply to the extremities such as hands and feet, depleting their supply of oxygen. Nicotine also increases the 'stickiness' of platelets, so raising the risk of thrombosis.

SAQ 4.8

Describe the effects of tobacco smoke on the cardio-vascular system.

Strokes

A stroke occurs when an artery in the brain bursts so that blood leaks into brain tissue (a brain haemorrhage) or, more likely, when there is a blockage due to atherosclerosis. The brain tissue in the area supplied by the artery is starved of oxygen and dies (a **cerebral infarction**). A comparison of healthy and dead brain tissue is shown in *figure 4.8*. The risk of a stroke is increased by high blood pressure; raised blood pressure may account for up to 60% of all strokes. Smoking causes an increase in blood pressure, often making an already bad situation worse.

Prevention and cure of coronary heart disease

Reducing the incidence of CHD is the first target listed in the British Government's long-term health strategy, *The Health of the Nation*. The reasons for this are that CHD is:

■ the major cause of premature death in the UK;
■ one of the main causes of avoidable ill health;
■ a major cost to the NHS and to the community.

Treatment for CHD involves using drugs to lower blood pressure, decrease the risk of blood clotting, prevent abnormal heart rhythms, reduce the retention of fluids and decrease the cholesterol concentration in the blood. If these drug treatments are not successful then a coronary artery **by-pass operation** may be carried out. This involves using a blood vessel from the leg to replace the diseased vessel. The by-pass carries blood from the aorta to a place on the heart beyond the blockage in the coronary artery. Sometimes two or three by-passes

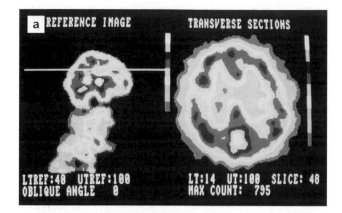

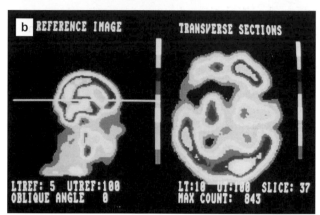

● *Figure 4.8* Scintigram scans of a normal brain and a brain following a stroke. Scintigram scanning shows the pattern of γ rays emitted by a radioactive tracer introduced into the body. The tracer is taken up by different tissues producing a distinct image in organs and tissues which are functioning correctly. **a** Scan of a normal brain in vertical and horizontal section. The white line on the left shows the position of the horizontal section. **b** Scan of a brain following a stroke. The black area in the front of the horizontal section shows where tissue has died as a result of an infarction.

are necessary. Coronary artery by-pass surgery is the most common method of surgery. The number of by-pass operations carried out in the UK increased threefold during the 1980s. In 1992 there were over 21 000 operations, compared with 140 heart transplants to treat CHD.

A heart transplant is the method of last resort. The costs of the operation are very high and there are difficulties in finding enough donor hearts. Before the operation can be carried out, the tissues of the donor and the recipient must be matched so that the new heart is not rejected by the body's immune system. Often heart–lung transplants are more successful than heart-only transplants, as the immune system seems to be 'overwhelmed' by the new organs and does not mount such a vigorous defence. Drugs are used to suppress the immune system after the transplant, but these often have unpleasant side-effects and may not prevent rejection. There is also the problem of deciding who receives a transplant. In some cases doctors have refused surgery to people who have ignored advice to give up smoking.

The new, and less invasive surgical method of **angioplasty** involves stretching coronary arteries by inserting a deflated balloon into the femoral artery in the leg, positioning it in the narrowed coronary artery and expanding the balloon several times. This technique does not require a general anaesthetic and may reduce the number of coronary artery by-pass operations in the future.

Treating CHD is a huge expense. Preventing the disease is much more cost effective. There are two ways of taking forward a preventative approach. Both involve primary health care, advising people to take precautions to avoid developing this disease. One way is to screen the population to find people who are at risk of developing CHD. The best methods are screening for high blood pressure and high blood cholesterol concentration, and monitoring the behaviour of the heart during exercise. Screening can be done by doctors on a regular basis and can be followed up with advice to those at risk to give up smoking, adopt a healthier diet and take more exercise. Studies show that methods of lowering blood pressure, such as reducing salt intake and using drugs, are effective. However, attempts to lower blood cholesterol by using drugs or changes in the diet (cutting down on fat intake) are not as successful. This suggests that although high blood cholesterol is a good predictor of CHD (*table 4.5*) it is probably more effective to screen the population for other risk factors such as smoking, obesity and blood pressure. Screening could concentrate on men over the age of 40 as they are a high risk group.

The second way of reducing the cost of treating CHD is to encourage the population to adopt a healthy lifestyle to reduce the risks of developing it. Advertising and health education from an early age may be able to play a large part in reducing illness and deaths from CHD. Encouraging people to engage in different forms of aerobic exercise is seen as an important aspect of the 'population approach' as it often leads to changes in diet and weight management, and may be associated with stopping smoking and reducing alcohol intake. Exercise is also one way of decreasing blood pressure. This 'population approach' may be more effective than screening individuals as it may cause the bell-shaped curves for such risk factors as blood pressure and blood cholesterol concentration to shift to the left (i.e. with fewer people at the high-risk end of the range). As the population average decreases, the number of people in the high risk categories also decreases. *The Health of the Nation* includes several targets for the reduction of CHD such as decreasing the intake of total fat and saturated fatty acids in the diet.

A major problem with health campaigns is that many people resist the advice they are given to reduce fat intake, give up smoking and take more exercise. Many do not heed this advice until it is too late. As CHD is a long-term degenerative diseases this advice should be given early. Degenerative changes in arteries have been seen in children as young as seven.

The mortality rate from heart disease and strokes in the UK began to decrease in the 1970s. This may have something to do with changing lifestyle, for example decreasing the intake of saturated fat and giving up smoking. However, some studies suggest that it might have more to do with better maternal nutrition. These studies show that:

- higher birthweight is associated with lower blood pressure in middle age;
- higher weight at one year of age is associated with a lower risk of diabetes and a low level in the blood of apolipoprotein B, the main component of LDLs.

It appears from this epidemiological evidence that better maternal nutrition in the early and middle part of the 20th century meant that later generations were better protected against heart disease. It may also explain why CHD is more common among manual workers than among the professional classes.

SAQ 4.9

Suggest ways in which governments can attempt to reduce the incidence of CHD and strokes.

SUMMARY

Tobacco smoke contains tar, carbon monoxide and nicotine.

Damage to the bronchioles and alveoli occur in chronic obstructive pulmonary diseases. In chronic bronchitis the airways are blocked by inflammation and infection; in emphysema the alveoli are destroyed reducing the surface area for gaseous exchange.

Tar contains carcinogens which cause changes in DNA in bronchial epithelial cells leading to the development of a bronchial carcinoma. This is lung cancer.

Carbon monoxide combines irreversibly with haemoglobin, reducing the oxygen carrying capacity of the blood.

Nicotine stimulates the nervous system, increasing heart rate and blood pressure.

Long-term smoking damages the cardiovascular system, contributing to the development of atherosclerosis and CHD.

Epidemiological and experimental evidence show a strong correlation between smoking and lung cancer; smokers also have an increased risk of developing CHD.

Primary health care can reduce morbidity and mortality from CHD and strokes. Screening for risk factors of CHD identifies the people at risk of CHD and strokes and allows early intervention to reduce their risks. Advertising and education can promote the benefits of exercise, not smoking, avoiding an excessive consumption of alcohol and eating a diet low in saturated fat. These alternatives to treatment and surgery may be more cost effective in the long-term, but they depend on people being willing to change their lifestyle.

Questions

1 Describe the likely appearance of the bronchial epithelium of a long-term heavy smoker. Explain the appearance you describe.

2 Summarise the evidence which links smoking with **a** lung cancer and **b** CHD.

3 Discuss the screening methods which could be used to identify people at risk of developing CHD.

4 Discuss the possible reasons for the global distribution of CHD.

5 Explain why governments are actively promoting ways of reducing CHD. Suggest ways in which health promotion may be improved.

Chapter five

Infectious diseases

By the end of this chapter you should be able to:

1 describe the causes of cholera, malaria, AIDS and TB;

2 explain how these diseases are transmitted and assess the importance of these diseases worldwide;

3 discuss the roles of social, economic and biological factors in the prevention and control of these diseases;

4 outline the role of chemotherapy, especially the use of antibiotics, in the treatment of infectious disease.

Worldwide importance of infectious diseases

The four infectious diseases described in this chapter are all of worldwide importance. They pose serious public health problems now and for the foreseeable future. Since 1940 much of the success in treating bacterial infectious diseases has been due to antibiotics. Now, due to their overuse, some bacteria are resistant to these antibiotics.

The four diseases described in the following pages are of current concern as they have increased in prevalence in recent years. **Tuberculosis (TB),** once thought to be nearly eradicated, has shown a resurgence and poses a considerable health risk to both developed and developing countries. A new strain of **cholera** appeared in 1992 to begin the eighth pandemic of the disease. **Malaria** has been on the increase since the 1970s and constitutes a serious risk to health in many tropical countries. **AIDS** was officially recognised in 1981, but the virus (**HIV**) was in human populations for many years before it was identified. The spread of HIV infection since the early 1980s has been exponential.

Infectious diseases are transmissible, or communicable, diseases. This means that pathogens spread from infected people to uninfected people. Some diseases spread directly from one person to another, as the pathogen cannot survive outside the human body. Others can survive in water, human food, faeces or animals (including insects) and are transmitted indirectly from person to person. Some people may spread a pathogen even though they do not have the disease themselves. Such people are symptomless **carriers** and it can be very difficult to trace them as the source of an infection.

These diseases know no boundaries. As a result of international travel it is possible for a person to become infected in Kinshasa, Zaire one day and be in Brussels the next. Tourists, business travellers, migrants, refugees and asylum seekers all represent a challenge to health authorities. There are few effective barriers to disease transmission and the means of treating and curing diseases are rapidly becoming obsolete.

Cholera

The features of cholera are given in *table 5.1*. It is caused by the bacterium *Vibrio cholerae (figure 5.1).*

Causative agent	*Vibrio cholerae*
Methods of transmission	food-borne, water-borne
Global distribution	Asia, Africa, Latin America
Incubation period	1–5 days
Site of action of pathogen	wall of small intestine
Clinical features	diarrhoea ('rice water'), loss of water and salts, dehydration, weakness
Method of diagnosis	microscopical analysis of faeces
Annual incidence worldwide	5.5 million
Annual mortality worldwide	120 000

● **Table 5.1** The features of cholera

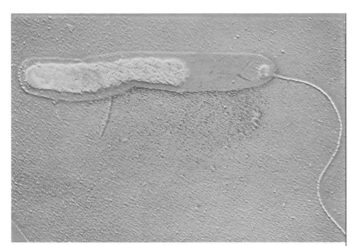

● *Figure 5.1* An electron micrograph of *Vibrio cholerae*. The faeces of a cholera victim are full of these bacteria with their distinctive flagella (× 22 500).

The disease occurs in parts of the world where people do not have access to proper sanitation, a clean water supply or uncontaminated food. Infected people, three quarters of whom may be symptomless carriers, pass out large numbers of bacteria in their faeces. If these contaminate the water supply, or if infected people handle food or cooking utensils without washing their hands, then bacteria are transmitted to uninfected people.

To reach the small intestine, bacteria have to pass through the stomach. If the contents are acid (< pH 4.5) the bacteria are unlikely to survive. If bacteria reach the small intestine they multiply and secrete a toxin, **choleragen**, which disrupts the functions of the epithelium so that salts and water leave the blood causing severe diarrhoea. This loss of fluid can be fatal if not treated within 24 hours.

Almost all people with cholera who are treated make a quick recovery. A death from cholera is an avoidable death. The disease can be controlled by giving a solution of salts and glucose intravenously to rehydrate the body *(figure 5.2)*. If people can drink they are given **oral rehydration therapy** *(ORT)*. Most cases of cholera are treated successfully with ORT. Glucose is effective because as it is absorbed into the blood it takes salts (e.g. Na$^+$ and K$^+$) with it. It is important to make sure that a sufferer's fluid intake equals fluid losses in urine and faeces and to maintain the osmotic balance of the blood and tissue fluids.

Cholera is almost unknown in the developed world as a result of sewage treatment and the provision of clean piped water, which is chlorinated to kill bacteria. The transmission cycle is broken. In developing countries, on the other hand, especially those with large cities which have grown considerably in recent years and have no sewage treatment or clean water, there exist perfect conditions for the spread of the disease. Increasing quantities of untreated faeces from a growing population favour cholera's survival. Many countries, saddled with huge debts, do not have the financial resources to tackle large municipal projects such as providing drainage and a clean water supply to large areas of substandard housing. In many countries raw human sewage is used to irrigate vegetables. This was the source of an outbreak in Santiago, Chile in 1991. Inadequate cooking or washing in contaminated water are other common causes.

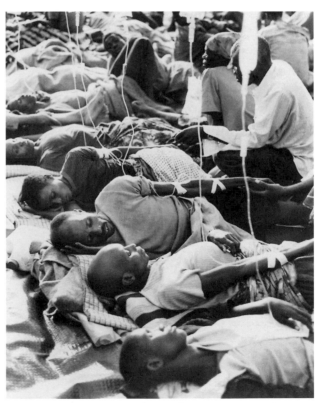

● *Figure 5.2* Refugees from the Rwandan civil war being treated for cholera with intravenous rehydration therapy. The drips contain a solution of salts (especially potassium) to replace those lost as a result of severe diarrhoea. Cholera claims many lives when normal life is disrupted as it is by war and other catastrophes.

Travellers to areas where cholera is endemic used to be advised to be vaccinated, although the vaccine only provides short-term protection. This recommendation has now largely been dropped. The reasons for this are explained in chapter 6.

There are 60 different strains of *V. cholerae*. Only the strain known as 01 causes cholera. Between 1817 and 1923 there were six pandemics of cholera. Each originated in the area now known as Bangladesh and they were caused by the 'classical' strain of cholera 01. A seventh pandemic began in 1961 when a variety of 01, named 'El Tor', originated in Indonesia. El Tor soon spread to India, then to Italy in 1973, reaching South America in January 1991 where it caused an epidemic in Peru. The discharge of a ship's sewage into the sea may have been responsible. Within days of the start of the epidemic the disease had spread 2000 km along the coast and within four weeks had moved inland. In February and March of that year, an average of 2550 cases a day were being reported. People in neighbouring countries were soon infected. In Peru, municipal waste systems are poorly maintained and chlorination of water supplies ineffective. Many sewers discharge straight onto shellfish beds. Seafood, especially filter-feeders such as oysters and mussels, become contaminated because they concentrate cholera bacteria when sewage is pumped into the sea. Fish and shellfish are often eaten raw. As the epidemic developed so rapidly in Peru, the disease probably spread through contaminated seafood.

A new strain, known as *V. cholerae* 0139, originated in Madras in October 1992 and has spread to other parts of India and Bangladesh. This strain threatens to be responsible for an eighth pandemic. It took El Tor 2 years to displace the 'classical' strain in India; 0139 replaced El Tor in less than two months suggesting that it may be more virulent. Many adult cases have been reported, and this may be because previous exposure to El Tor has not given them immunity to 0139.

SAQ 5.1
List the ways in which cholera is transmitted from person to person.

SAQ 5.2
One person can excrete 10^{13} cholera bacteria a day. An infective dose is 10^6. How many people could one person infect in one day?

SAQ 5.3
Explain why there is such a high risk of cholera in refugee camps.

SAQ 5.4
Describe the precautions that a visitor to a country where cholera is endemic can take to avoid catching the disease.

Malaria

Malaria is caused by one of four species of the protoctist *Plasmodium*, whose life cycle is shown in *figure 5.3*. The features of the disease are summarised in *table 5.2*.

Female *Anopheles* mosquitoes feed on human blood to obtain the protein they need to develop

Causative agent	*Plasmodium falciparum, P. vivax, P. ovale, P. malariae*
Method of transmission	insect vector: female *Anopheles* mosquito
Global distribution	throughout the tropics (endemic in 91 countries)
Incubation period	a week to a year
Site of action of pathogen	liver, red blood cells, brain
Clinical features	fever, anaemia, nausea, headaches, muscle pain, shivering, sweating, enlarged spleen
Method of diagnosis	microscopical examination of blood
Annual incidence worldwide	500 million (90% of cases are in Africa)
Annual mortality worldwide	up to 2.7 million; in tropical Africa malaria kills 1 million children under the age of 5

● *Table 5.2* The features of malaria

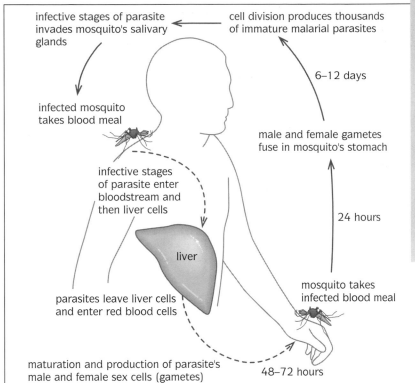

infective stages of parasite invades mosquito's salivary glands

cell division produces thousands of immature malarial parasites

6–12 days

infected mosquito takes blood meal

male and female gametes fuse in mosquito's stomach

infective stages of parasite enter bloodstream and then liver cells

24 hours

liver

parasites leave liver cells and enter red blood cells

mosquito takes infected blood meal

maturation and production of parasite's male and female sex cells (gametes)

48–72 hours

● *Figure 5.3* The life cycle of *Plasmodium*. The parasite has two hosts: the sexual stage occurs in mosquitoes, the asexual stage in humans. The time between infection and appearance of parasites inside red blood cells is 7 to 30 days in *P. falciparum*; longer in other species.

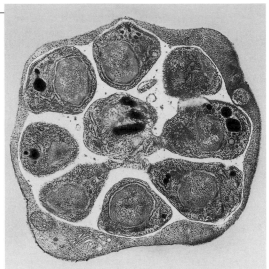

● *Figure 5.4* A transmission electron micrograph of a section through a red blood cell packed tightly with malarial parasites. *Plasmodium* multiplies inside red blood cells; this cell will soon burst releasing parasites which will infect other red blood cells.

their eggs. Mosquitoes transmit *Plasmodium* when they feed on an infected human host and absorb the parasite's gametes. These fuse and develop in the mosquito's gut to form infective stages, which move to the mosquito's salivary glands. When the mosquito feeds again the infective stages pass out into the blood together with an anticoagulant in the saliva. The parasites enter the red blood cells, where they multiply (*figure 5.4*). The female *Anopheles* mosquito is therefore a vector of malaria and she transmits the disease when she passes the infective stages into an uninfected person. Malaria may also be transmitted during blood transfusion and when unsterile needles are reused. *Plasmodium* can also pass across the placenta from mother to fetus.

Plasmodium multiplies in both hosts; at each stage there is a huge increase in the number of parasites and this improves the chances of infecting either a mosquito or a human host.

When people are continually reinfected they become immune to malaria. However, this only happens if they survive the first five years of life when mortality from malaria is very high. The immunity only lasts as long as they are in contact with the disease. This explains why epidemics in places where malaria is not endemic can be very serious, and why it is more dangerous in those areas where it only occurs during and after the rainy season. This often coincides with the time of maximum agricultural activity so the disease has a disastrous effect on the economy: people cannot cultivate the land when they are sick.

Over the past few years *Anopheles* mosquitoes have spread because mosquito control programmes have been abandoned throughout the tropics as a result of civil war and the disruption of civil administration. The reasons for the worldwide concern over the spread of malaria are:

■ an increase in drug-resistant forms of *Plasmodium*;

■ an increase in the proportion of cases caused by *P. falciparum*, the form that causes severe, often fatal malaria;

■ difficulties in developing a vaccine.

There are three main ways to control malaria:

1 reduce the number of mosquitoes;
2 avoid being bitten by mosquitoes;
3 use drugs to prevent the parasite infecting people.

It is possible to kill the insect vector and break the transmission cycle. Mosquitoes lay their eggs in water. Larvae hatch and develop in water but breathe air by coming to the surface. Oil can be spread over the surfaces of water to make it impossible for mosquito larvae and pupae to breathe. Marshes can be drained and vegetation cleared. Two biological control measures that can be used are:

■ stocking ponds, irrigation and drainage ditches and other permanent bodies of water with fish which feed on mosquito larvae;
■ spraying a preparation containing the bacterium *Bacillus thuringiensis*, which kills mosquito larvae, but is not toxic to other forms of life.

Mosquitoes will lay their eggs in small puddles or pools and this makes it impossible to eradicate breeding sites, especially in the rainy season.

The best protection against malaria is to avoid being bitten. People are advised to sleep beneath mosquito nets and use insect repellents. Soaking mosquito nets in insecticide every six months has been shown to reduce mortality from malaria. People should not expose their skin when mosquitoes are active at dusk. Villagers in New Guinea recommend sleeping with a dog or a pig. They say that mosquitoes much prefer animal blood to human blood.

Anti-malarial drugs such as quinine and chloroquine are used to treat infected people. They are used as **prophylactic** (preventative) drugs, stopping an infection occurring if a person is bitten by an infected mosquito. They are taken before, during and after visiting an area where malaria is endemic. One such drug, chloroquine, inhibits protein synthesis and prevents the parasite spreading within the body. Another prophylactic, proguanil, has the added advantage of inhibiting the sexual reproduction of *Plasmodium* inside the biting mosquito. Where anti-malarial drugs have been used widely there are strains of drug-resistant

Plasmodium. Chloroquine resistance is widespread in East Africa and New Guinea. Some drugs have unpleasant side effects such as restlessness, dizziness, vomiting and disturbed sleep.

People visiting the tropics are at great risk of contracting malaria. There were between 1500 and 2300 cases of malaria a year in the UK between 1984 and 1993. Doctors in developed countries, who see very few cases of malaria, often misdiagnose it as influenza since the initial symptoms are similar. Many of these cases are settled immigrants who have returned to Africa or India to visit relatives. They do not take prophylactic drugs, because they do not realise that they have lost their immunity.

In the 1950s the World Health Organisation coordinated a worldwide eradication programme. Although malaria was cleared from some countries, it was not generally successful. There were two main reasons for this:

1 *Plasmodium* became resistant to the drugs used to control it.
2 Mosquitoes became resistant to DDT and the other insecticides that were used at the time, such as dieldrin.

This programme was also hugely expensive and often unpopular. People living in areas where malaria was temporarily eradicated by the programme lost their immunity and suffered considerably, even dying, when the disease returned. Some villagers in South-East Asia lost the roofs of their houses because dieldrin killed a parasitic wasp that controlled the numbers of thatch-eating caterpillars. Some spray teams were set upon and killed by angry villagers in New Guinea. The programme could have been more successful if it had been tackled more sensitively with the aims of the programme explained to people. In the 1970s, war and civil unrest destroyed much of the infrastructure throughout Africa and South-East Asia, making it impossible for mosquito control teams to work effectively.

SAQ 5.5

Describe how malaria is transmitted.

SAQ 5.6

Describe the factors that make malaria a difficult disease to control.

SAQ 5.7

Describe the precautions that people can take to avoid catching malaria.

Acquired Immune Deficiency Syndrome (AIDS)

AIDS is caused by the human immunodeficiency virus (HIV) *(figure 5.5)*. Features of AIDS and HIV are listed in *table 5.3*. The virus infects and destroys cells of the body's immune system *(figure 5.6)* so that their numbers gradually decrease. These cells, known as T lymphocytes (see page 69), control the immune system's response to infection. When the numbers are low the body is unable to defend itself against infection, so allowing a range of parasites to cause a variety of different infections (known as opportunistic infections). AIDS is

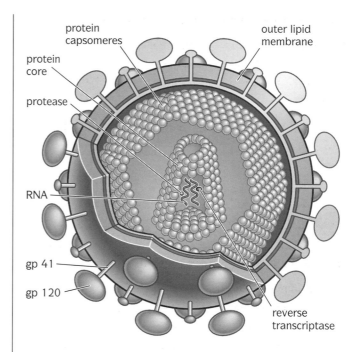

● **Figure 5.5** Human immunodeficiency virus (HIV). The outer envelope contains two glycoproteins gp120 and gp 41. The protein core contains the genetic material (RNA) and two enzymes, protease and reverse transcriptase. Reverse transcriptase uses the RNA as a template to produce DNA once the virus is inside a host cell.

Causative agent	Human Immunodeficiency virus (HIV-1 and HIV-2)
Methods of transmission	in semen and vaginal fluids during sexual intercourse, infected blood or blood products, contaminated hypodermic syringes, mother to fetus across placenta, mother to infant in breast milk
Global distribution	worldwide, especially in Africa and South-East Asia
Incubation period	initial incubation a few weeks, but up to ten years or more before symptoms of AIDS develop
Site of action of pathogen	T helper lymphocytes, macrophages, brain cells
Clinical features	HIV infection – flu-like symptoms and then symptomless; AIDS – opportunistic infections including pneumonia, TB, and cancers; weight loss, diarrhoea, fever, sweating, mental diseases
Method of diagnosis	test for antibodies to HIV
Estimated total number of people infected with HIV worldwide in 1995	20 million adults
Estimated number of cases of AIDS worldwide in 1994	4 million
Estimated number of deaths from AIDS-related diseases worldwide in 1995	1 million (one third due to TB)

● **Table 5.3** The features of HIV/AIDS

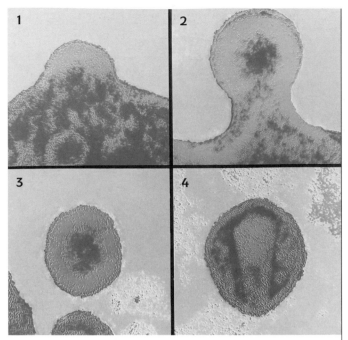

● *Figure 5.6* A series of transmission electron micrographs showing HIV budding from the surface of an infected lymphocyte. The viral particle first appears as a bump (1) which then buds out (2) and is eventually cut off from the cell membrane of the host cell (3). The outer shell of dense material and less dense core are visible in the released virus (4).

not a disease. It is a collection of these rare opportunistic diseases associated with immunodeficiency caused by HIV infection. Since HIV is an infective agent, AIDS is called an 'acquired' immunodeficiency to distinguish it from other types, for example an inherited form.

The World Health Organisation estimated in 1995 that 20 million adults had been infected with HIV since the beginning of the pandemic. By 2000 there may be 30–40 million infected people, 90% of them in developing countries. In 1994, 1 million new cases of AIDS were reported. The statistics below show how grave the pandemic is in Africa alone.

■ Equal numbers of males and females are HIV+ as transmission is via heterosexual contact.

■ One third of the adult population in Uganda is infected with HIV.

■ 35% of hospital admissions in one hospital in central Africa had HIV.

■ 2 million adults are estimated to have AIDS.

■ 10 million people are thought to be infected with HIV.

■ It is estimated that HIV will leave 10 million orphans.

■ The prevalence of HIV among women attending antenatal clinics in South Africa increased by 300% from 1990 to 1992.

■ Blood transfusions have been responsible for 10% of HIV infections in adults, and 30% in children.

■ There is a 30–45% risk of transmission from mothers to their children.

■ 35% of TB patients are HIV+; 30% of AIDS patients die of TB.

SAQ 5.8

Suggest why the true total of AIDS cases worldwide may be much higher than reported.

HIV is a virus that is spread by intimate human contact: there is no vector and the virus is unable to survive outside the human body. Sexual intercourse is the main method of transmission. The initial epidemic in North America and Europe was amongst male homosexuals who had many sex partners and practised anal intercourse. The mucous lining of the rectum is not as thick as that lining the vagina. It is often damaged during intercourse and the virus passes from semen to blood. As many homosexuals were blood donors and also had heterosexual relationships, the virus spread more widely. At high risk of infection were haemophiliacs who were treated with a clotting substance (factor 8) isolated from blood pooled from many donors. The transmission of HIV by heterosexual transmission is rising in developed countries. In Africa it has always been transmitted in this way, which explains the equal numbers of males and females who are HIV+ ('HIV positive').

SAQ 5.9

Children in Africa with sickle cell disease and malaria often receive blood transfusions. Explain how this puts them at risk of HIV infection.

HIV infects the cells of the lymphoid system. It is a slow virus and after a first infection there may not be any symptoms until between two and ten or more years later. Some people who have the virus appear not to develop any initial symptoms, although there are often flu-like symptoms for several weeks after becoming infected. Over several years the immune system collapses and the body is attacked by opportunistic infections. Two of these are caused by fungi: oral thrush caused by *Candida albicans*, and a rare form of pneumonia caused by *Pneumocystis carinii*. During the early years of the epidemic people in developed countries died within twelve hours of contracting this unusual pneumonia. Now this condition is managed much better and drugs are prescribed to prevent the disease developing. As the immune system collapses, it becomes less effective in finding and destroying cancers. A rare form of cancer, Kaposi's sarcoma caused by a herpes-like virus, is associated with AIDS. Kaposi's sarcoma and cancers of internal organs are now most likely to cause the death of people with AIDS in developed countries.

At about the same time that AIDS was first reported on the west coast of the USA and in Europe, doctors in Central Africa reported seeing people with similar opportunistic infections. HIV infection is now widespread throughout sub-Saharan Africa from Uganda to South Africa. It is a serious public health problem here because HIV infection compounds existing diseases such as malnutrition, TB and malaria. AIDS is having an adverse effect on the economic development of countries in the region as it affects sexually active people in their twenties and thirties who are also the most economically productive.

There is no cure for AIDS and there is as yet no vaccine for HIV. No-one knows how many people with HIV will progress to developing AIDS. Some people think it is 100%. Drug therapy can slow down the onset of AIDS, but the drugs are expensive and have a variety of side effects. If used in combination, two drugs which prevent the replication of the virus inside host cells can prolong life, but they do not offer a cure. The drugs are similar to DNA nucleotides (e.g. zidovudine is similar to

the nucleotide which has the base thymine). Zidovudine binds to the viral enzyme reverse transcriptase and blocks its action. This stops the replication of the viral genetic material and leads to an increase in T lymphocytes.

The spread of AIDS is difficult to control. The virus has a long latent stage when it can be transmitted by people who are HIV+ but who show no symptoms of AIDS. It is mainly spread by sexual activity, but is also transmitted across the placenta and in breast milk from one generation to the next. The virus changes its surface proteins, which makes it hard for the body's immune system to counteract it. This also makes the development of a vaccine very difficult.

For the present, public health measures are the only way to stop the spread of HIV. People are educated about the spread of the infection and encouraged to change their behaviour. The condom and the femidom are the only effective methods of reducing the risk of infection during intercourse as they form a barrier between the body fluids, reducing the chances of transmission of the virus.

SAQ 5.10

Suggest why condoms are not fully effective at preventing HIV infection.

SAQ 5.11

Suggest the types of advice which might be offered as part of an AIDS education programme.

Contact tracing is an important part of HIV control in the UK. If a person who is diagnosed as HIV+ is willing (or able) to identify the people who they have put at risk of infection by sexual intercourse or needle sharing, then these people will be offered an HIV test. This test identifies the presence of antibodies to HIV. These only appear several weeks after the initial infection.

Injecting drug users are advised to give up their habit, stop sharing needles or take their drug in some other way. Needle exchange schemes operate in some places to exchange used needles for sterile ones to reduce the chances of infection with HIV and other blood-borne diseases *(figure 7.3)*.

In developed countries, blood collected from blood donors is routinely screened for HIV and heat-treated to kill any viruses. People who think they may have been exposed to the virus are discouraged from donating blood. Both methods are expensive and unlikely to be implemented throughout the developing world for some time. In these countries, people about to have an operation are recommended to donate their own blood before surgery to reduce the risk of infection.

Widespread testing of a population to find people who are HIV+ is not expensive, but governments are reluctant to introduce such testing because of the infringement of personal freedom. In the

West, HIV testing is concentrated on people in high risk groups, such as homosexuals, prostitutes, injecting drug users and their sexual partners. If tested positive they can be given the medical and psychological support they need. In Africa and South-East Asia the epidemic is not restricted to such easily identifiable groups and widespread testing is not feasible due to the expense of reaching the majority of the population and the difficulty of organising it. People in these regions find out that they are HIV+ when they develop the symptoms of AIDS.

SAQ 5.12

Explain why the early identification of HIV+ people is important in transmission control.

HIV+ women in developed countries are advised not to breast feed their children because of the risk of transmitting the virus to their child. Both viral particles and infected lymphocytes are found in breast milk. In developing countries the benefits of breast feeding, such as the protection this gives against other diseases, outweigh the risks of transmitting HIV.

Tuberculosis

Tuberculosis (TB) is caused by two bacteria, *Mycobacterium tuberculosis (figure 5.7)* and *M. bovis*. The disease spreads when infected people with the active form of the illness cough or sneeze. It spreads most rapidly among people living in overcrowded conditions. *M. bovis* causes TB in cattle and is spread to humans in meat and milk. It is estimated that there were about 800 000 deaths in the UK between 1850 and 1950 as a result of TB transmitted from cattle. However, most people with TB are infected with *M. tuberculosis*. They have a persistent cough and, as part of their defence, cells release hormone-like compounds which cause fever and suppress the appetite. As a result sufferers lose weight and often look emaciated *(figure 5.8)*. *Table 5.4* gives the main features of the disease.

The incidence of TB in the UK decreased steeply well before the introduction of a vaccine in the 1950s, because of improvements in housing conditions and diet. The antibiotic streptomycin was introduced in the 1940s and this hastened the decrease in incidence of TB. This pattern was repeated throughout the developed world.

Once thought to be practically eradicated, TB is now showing a resurgence. This is due in part to the following factors:

■ some strains of TB bacteria which are resistant to drugs;
■ the AIDS pandemic;
■ poor housing and rising homelessness in inner cities in the developed world;

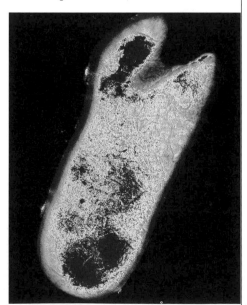

● *Figure 5.7* A transmission electron micrograph of *Mycobacterium tuberculosis*. It is surrounded by a thick layer of lipids which make it difficult to kill with drugs. The cell wall has split, as happens when it is killed by antibiotics. (× 60 000)

Causative agents	*Mycobacterium tuberculosis; M. bovis*
Methods of transmission	airborne droplets; via unpasteurised milk
Global distribution	worldwide
Incubation period	few weeks or months
Site of action of pathogen	primary infection in lungs; secondary infections in lymph nodes, bones and gut
Clinical features	racking cough, coughing blood, chest pain, shortness of breath, fever, sweating, weight loss
Methods of diagnosis	Microscopical examination of sputum for bacteria, chest X-ray
Annual incidence worldwide in 1995	9 million (5000 cases in UK)
Annual mortality worldwide in 1995	3 million

● **Table 5.4** The features of tuberculosis

■ the breakdown of TB control programmes particularly in the USA; partial treatment for TB increases the chance of drug resistance in *Mycobacterium*.

TB attacks many of the poorest and socially disadvantaged because it is spread by airborne droplets and people who sleep close together in large numbers are particularly at risk. The disease primarily attacks the homeless and people who live in poor, substandard housing, and for this reason was prevalent in the 19th century. Those with low immunity, because of malnutrition or being HIV+, are also particularly vulnerable.

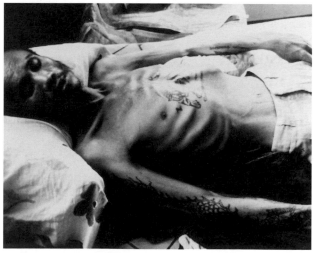

● **Figure 5.8** A TB patient in Thailand. Health workers or members of his family may supervise his drug treatment which can last for up to a year.

In 1995, TB killed more people worldwide than any other disease. It is estimated that one third of the world's population is infected with *M. tuberculosis*. It is attacked by the macrophages in the lungs, but is not killed. It is predicted that 300 million people may become infected within the next 10 years and, without treatment, each person may infect 10 to 15 others every year.

Transmission is easily achieved and the bacteria may remain in the lungs, or in the lymphoid tissue, for years until they become active.

TB is often the first opportunistic infection to strike HIV+ people. HIV infection may reactivate dormant infections of *M. tuberculosis*. TB is now the leading cause of death of HIV+ people. The HIV pandemic has been followed very closely by a TB pandemic. There are high rates of incidence all across the developing world and in the countries of the former Soviet Union *(figure 5.9)*. Very high rates are also found in areas of destitution in developed countries, where the incidence in parts of some inner cities is as high as in countries like Tanzania. The recent epidemic of TB in the USA happened as a result of neglect and poverty, especially in parts of New York where the public health system almost collapsed. Social factors, such as homelessness, neglect of primary health care and urban decay, contributed to the spread of TB and these need to be addressed if the pandemic is to be curbed.

Once someone appears with the symptoms of TB, the sputum (mucus and pus) from their lungs

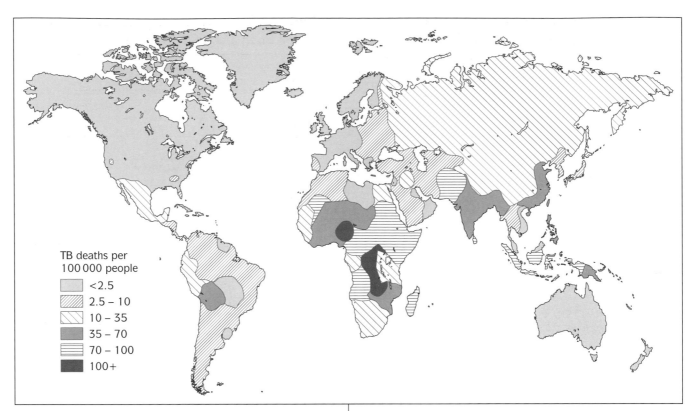

● *Figure 5.9* The global distribution of TB.

is collected for analysis. The identification of *M. tuberculosis* can be made very quickly by microscopy. If TB is confirmed, then sufferers should be isolated while they are in the most infectious stage (which is at two to four weeks). This is particularly the case if they have an infection of a drug-resistant strain. The treatment involves using several drugs to ensure that all the bacteria are killed, not just a few. Otherwise, drug resistant forms are left behind to continue the infection. The treatment is a long one (six months to one year), but many people do not complete their course of drugs as they think that when they feel better they are cured. However, it takes months to kill mycobacteria because they are slow growing. They are intracellular parasites surviving inside cells of the immune system, where they are metabolically inactive and therefore difficult to treat with drugs.

Strains of drug-resistant *M. tuberculosis* were identified when treatment with antibiotics, such as streptomycin, began in the 1950s. Antibiotics act as selective agents killing drug-sensitive strains and leaving resistant ones behind. Drug resistance

happens as a result of mutation. This is a random event occurring with a frequency of once in every 1000 bacteria. If three or four drugs are used in treatment then the chance of resistance occurring to all of them is reduced to $(1/1000)^3$ or $(1/1000)^4$. If TB is not treated or the person stops the treatment before the bacteria are completely eliminated, bacteria spread throughout the body increasing the likelihood that mutations will arise. Prematurely stopping treatment can mean that *M. tuberculosis* develops resistance to all the drugs being used. Patients under poorly managed treatment programmes return home to infect others.

Multiple drug resistant forms of TB (MDR-TB) now exist. In 1995 an HIV unit in London reported an outbreak of MDR-TB with a form of *M. tuberculosis* that was resistant to five of the major drugs used to treat the disease including isoniazid, the most successful.

The World Health Organisation promotes a scheme to ensure that patients complete their course of drugs. DOTS (Direct Observation Treatment, Short Course), involves health workers, or responsible family members, making sure that patients take their medicine regularly for six to eight months. The drugs widely used are isoniazid and rifampicin, often in combination with others. This drug therapy cures 95% of all patients and is twice as effective as other strategies, helping to reduce the spread of MDR strains.

Contact tracing (see page 59) and the subsequent testing of contacts for the bacterium is an essential part of controlling TB. Contacts are screened for symptoms of TB infection, but the diagnosis can take up to two weeks. The spread of the disease among children is prevented, to a large extent, by vaccination. The BCG vaccine is derived from *M. bovis* and protects up to 70 to 80% of teenagers in the UK, its effectiveness decreasing with age unless there is exposure to TB. Studies of the effectiveness of BCG in protecting adults and children give conflicting results. It appears that the vaccine is effective in some parts of the world (eg UK) and less effective in others (eg India). Many of the world's TB victims were not vaccinated.

An effective method of control is the dual approach of milk pasteurisation and TB-testing of cattle. Any cattle found to test positive are destroyed. These measures have reduced the incidence of TB caused by *M. bovis* considerably, so that it is hardly a hazard to health in countries where these controls operate. In 1995 there were just eleven cases of TB caused by *M. bovis* in the UK.

SAQ 5.13(a)
Describe the global distribution of TB.

SAQ 5.13(b)
Explain the reasons for the distribution you have described.

Chemotherapy and antibiotics

Chemotherapy is the use of drugs to treat or cure infections. Effective drugs show selective toxicity, killing the pathogen but having no effect on host cells. There is a wide range of chemotherapeutic agents for bacterial and fungal infections, but few for viral infections. Some drugs are derived from natural compounds but others, such as isoniazid used for the treatment of tuberculosis, are synthetic.

SAQ 5.14
Suggest why there are few anti-viral drugs.

Antibiotics are natural chemotherapeutic agents made by microorganisms. In dilute solution they inhibit the growth of, or kill, other microorganisms. Many antibiotics are modified chemically to increase their effectiveness. They interfere with some aspect of growth or metabolism of the target organism such as:

- synthesis of bacterial walls;
- protein synthesis (transcription and translation);
- cell membrane function;
- enzyme action.

Penicillins function by preventing the synthesis of the cross links between the peptidoglycan polymers in the cell wall. This means that they are only active against bacteria which are growing. Many types of bacteria have enzymes for destroying penicillins (penicillinases) and are therefore resistant to the antibiotic. The main sites of action of antibiotics are shown in *figure 5.10*.

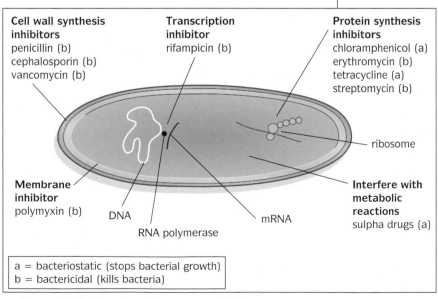

Cell wall synthesis inhibitors
penicillin (b)
cephalosporin (b)
vancomycin (b)

Transcription inhibitor
rifampicin (b)

Protein synthesis inhibitors
chloramphenicol (a)
erythromycin (b)
tetracycline (a)
streptomycin (b)

ribosome

Membrane inhibitor
polymyxin (b)

DNA

RNA polymerase

mRNA

Interfere with metabolic reactions
sulpha drugs (a)

a = bacteriostatic (stops bacterial growth)
b = bactericidal (kills bacteria)

● *Figure 5.10* The sites of action of antibiotics.

SAQ 5.15

Suggest why the different types of antibiotic shown in *figure 5.10* do not kill human cells.

Different diseases are treated with different antibiotics. All strains of some bacteria are resistant to several antibiotics. For example, *M. tuberculosis* is resistant to penicillin. **Broad spectrum antibiotics** are effective against a wide range of bacteria; narrow spectrum only against a few.

Antibiotics should be chosen carefully. Screening antibiotics against the strain of the bacterium or fungus isolated from sufferers ensures that the most effective antibiotic can be chosen. *Figure 5.11* shows the results of an antibiotic sensitivity test carried out on a strain of the human gut bacterium *Escherichia coli* that causes epidemics of food-borne and water-borne infections. Bacteria are collected from faeces, or from food or water, and grown on an agar medium. Different antibiotics are absorbed onto discs of filter paper and placed on the agar plate. The plate is incubated and the

diameters of the inhibition zones where no bacteria are growing are measured. The diameters are compared with a table similar to *table 5.5* and the most appropriate antibiotics are chosen to treat infected people.

SAQ 5.16

Which of the antibiotics in *figure 5.11*/*table 5.5* would be chosen to treat the patient with the pathogenic strain of *E. coli*? Explain your answer.

Increasingly, bacteria which were once susceptible to antibiotics are becoming resistant. This has a great impact on disease control as it prolongs epidemics, lengthening the period of time when people are ill and increasing the risk of higher mortality rates. The inappropriate and widespread use of antibiotics should therefore be discouraged. Some drugs should be kept for use as a 'last resort' when everything else has failed, and drug companies must continue to invest in research for new drugs to replace those which quickly become redundant.

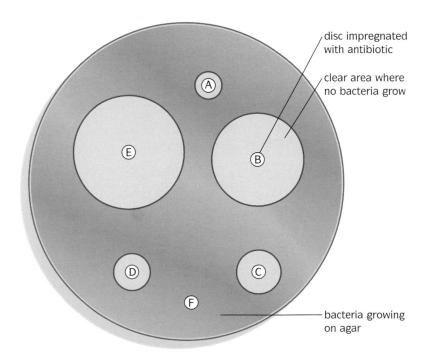

● **Figure 5.11** An antibiotic sensitivity test for a pathogenic strain of *Escherichia coli*. *Table 5.5* shows the inhibition zone diameters for the six antibiotics.

Antibiotic	Inhibition zone diameter/mm	
	Resistant	*Sensitive*
A	≤11	≥14
B	≤12	≥18
C	≤ 9	≥14
D	≤11	≥22
E	≤12	≥15
F	≤14	≥19

If the diameter of the inhibition zone for an antibiotic is equal to or less than the figure given in the first column, the bacteria are resistant to it. If the diameter is equal to or greater than the figure in the right hand column, they are sensitive and the antibiotic may be chosen for chemotherapy.

● **Table 5.5** Inhibition zone diameters for the antibiotics of *figure 5.11*

SUMMARY

Cholera is caused by the bacterium *Vibrio cholerae* and is transmitted in water or food contaminated by the faeces of infected people.

Malaria is caused by four species of *Plasmodium*. The most dangerous is *P. falciparum*. The disease is transmitted by female *Anopheles* mosquitoes that transfer *Plasmodium* from infected to uninfected people.

AIDS is a set of diseases caused by the destruction of the immune system by infection with human immunodeficiency virus (HIV). HIV is transmitted in certain body fluids: blood, semen, vaginal secretions and breast milk. It also crosses the placenta. It primarily infects economically active members of populations in developing countries and has an adverse effect on social and economic development.

TB is caused by the bacterium *Mycobacterium tuberculosis* (in developing countries, it may also be caused by *M. bovis*, which also causes a related disease in cattle).

Cholera, malaria, AIDS and TB are all increasing in prevalence and pose severe threats to the health of populations in developed and developing countries.

Public health measures are taken to reduce the transmission of the diseases, but to be effective they must be informed by a knowledge of the life cycle of each pathogen.

Antibiotics are natural chemotherapeutic agents produced by microorganisms and are used to inhibit the growth of pathogenic organisms. Most are only effective against bacteria. The widespread and indiscriminate use of antibiotics has led to growth of resistant strains of bacteria. This poses a serious challenge to the maintenance of health services in the 21st century.

Questions

1 Describe the transmission of cholera, malaria, tuberculosis and HIV/AIDS.

2 Discuss the public health measures that should be taken during a cholera epidemic.

3 Explain how a knowledge of the life cycle of the malarial parasite is important in devising methods to control the spread of the disease.

4 Describe how you would attempt to prevent the spread of malaria in a rural community in the tropics.

5 Explain the value of the following in disease control: contact tracing, DOTS for TB, antibiotic sensitivity tests, isolation of patients and health education.

6 Discuss the social, biological and economic problems associated with controlling the spread of HIV infection.

7 Outline the role of antibiotics in controlling disease.

8 Discuss the social, medical and economic problems of controlling the spread of disease in sub-Saharan Africa.

Immunity

Defence against disease

Measles is caused by a virus which enters the body and replicates inside human cells. There are no symptoms for about 8 to 14 days and then a rash appears and a fever develops. In children, after about ten days the disease clears up and there are rarely any complications. Measles used to be a common childhood disease in the UK that most people had only once. Amongst poor people, especially in overcrowded conditions, measles is a serious disease and a major cause of death especially among infants. In most cases it is very unlikely that anyone surviving the disease will suffer from it again. They are immune. While suffering from the symptoms of the disease the body's defence system has developed a way of recognising the virus and preventing it from doing any harm again. **Immunity** is the protection against disease provided by the body's defence or immune system. There are two parts to this system:

- the **non-specific system**;
- the **specific system**.

Many pathogens do not harm the body because we have physical, chemical and cellular defences that prevent them from entering or, if they do enter, from spreading through the body. These defences, present from birth, form the **non-specific system**. This system does not distinguish between different pathogens and gives the same response each time the same pathogen attacks.

The **specific system** gives a highly effective, long-lasting immunity to anything the body recognises as foreign. Specialised cells, known as **lymphocytes,** direct a defence against specific pathogens. Although highly efficient, this specific immune response is slow when it encounters a pathogen for the first time. During the first encounter some lymphocytes produce special protein molecules, called **antibodies**, which are targeted specifically at the invading pathogen. Although the capability to produce antibodies is present from before birth, they are only produced when the appropriate pathogen invades.

The specific immune system recognises pathogens because their surfaces are covered in large molecules such as proteins, glycoproteins and polysaccharides. In addition, the immune system recognises as foreign the compounds, such as toxins, which some pathogens produce. Any molecule which the body recognises as foreign is an **antigen**. The second and any further encounters with the same pathogen are met by a much more rapid and effective response, which prevents invasion or spread through the body.

The human immune system is distributed throughout the body and includes many tissues and organs, such as the stomach and the epidermis of the skin. The main features of the immune system are shown in *table 6.1*. Keep referring to this table as you read the rest of this chapter.

Feature	Non-specific immune system	Specific immune system
tissues and organs	epidermis of skin, mucous membranes, ciliated epithelia	lymphoid tissues in lymph nodes, gut, trachea, lungs and bronchi, spleen
cell types	mast cells, phagocytes (neutrophils and macrophages)	lymphocytes (T cells and B cells)
molecules produced	histamine, lysozyme, plasma proteins (complement proteins, acute phase proteins), interferons	antibodies and cytokines secreted by lymphocytes
resistance to disease	unchanged by repeated infections	improved by repeated infection (immunological memory)
specificity	non-specific: equally effective against all pathogens	specific to invading pathogen, slow to respond to new infections

● **Table 6.1** The features of the non-specific and specific immune systems

SAQ 6.1

a Explain, in simple terms, why people do not usually catch measles twice.

b Explain the terms *antigen* and *antibody*.

Non-specific immunity

The surface of the skin is composed of layers of dead cells, which bacteria, viruses and fungi cannot penetrate. It is a physical barrier. The only way in which these pathogens can enter the body through the skin is via cuts, wounds and abrasions. Some external parasites such as lice, fleas, ticks, bed bugs and mosquitoes puncture the skin to feed on blood. Most of these are vectors of disease, for example *Anopheles* mosquitoes carry *Plasmodium*, which causes malaria; tsetse flies carry trypanosomes, which cause sleeping sickness; some fleas carry the bacterium *Yersinia pestis*, which causes bubonic plague. Larger parasites such as hookworm enter by penetrating the skin.

Most pathogens enter the body through the linings of the gas exchange system, alimentary canal and urinary and genital tracts. These are protected by layers of epithelial cells covered in a layer of protective mucus. When bacteria invade the body they often grow on the mucus that covers epithelia. Some, such as *Vibrio cholerae*, remain there and do not penetrate further. Others penetrate epithelia and grow vigorously inside the body. There they may attack cells and release toxins. Viruses enter through mucous membranes and travel through the blood to tissues which they infect. Some only travel a short distance, for example the influenza virus infects cells lining the trachea and lungs, but the polio virus travels further to reach nerve cells. Some viruses bind to cell membrane proteins and are taken into the cytoplasm by endocytosis. Once inside, viruses direct the protein-synthetic machinery of the cell towards the production of new viral particles, or become dormant.

Cells of the immune system

The cells of the immune system originate from **stem cells** in the bone marrow *(figure 6.2)*. Stem cells retain the ability to divide by mitosis forming large numbers of cells which differentiate into specialised cells. There are two groups of these cells involved in defence:

1 phagocytes: neutrophils and macrophages;
2 lymphocytes.

Phagocytes

Phagocytes are continually produced by bone marrow throughout life. They are stored there and leave in the blood to be distributed around the body. They are scavengers and are involved in the non-specific response *(table 6.1)*.

Neutrophils form about 60% of the white cells in the blood. They are smaller than macrophages and travel throughout the body. Their numbers increase rapidly during an infection, when they are released from stores in bone marrow. Neutrophils pass from the blood to the tissues by squeezing through capillary walls (*figure 6.6*). They are short-lived cells.

Macrophages circulate in the blood and pass into organs such as the lungs, liver, spleen, kidney and lymph nodes, where they tend to remain. They are large, long-lived cells which remove foreign matter from organs such as the lungs (*figure 3.5c*). They play a crucial role in initiating the specific immune response to infection by pathogens.

SAQ 6.2 _____

Suggest reasons for the distribution of *secondary* lymphoid tissue shown in *figure 6.1*.

Lymphocytes

Lymphocytes are produced before birth and leave the bone marrow to fill the lymphoid system. They are generally not phagocytic, but

Box 6A The lymphoid system

Lymphoid tissue is found throughout the body. It consist of all the areas that contain lymphocytes and make antibodies. These areas are joined together by small vein-like vessels called **lymphatic vessels**. Some areas of lymphoid tissue are quite distinct such as the spleen and the lymph nodes in the groin. In the lungs and the gut, lymphoid tissue is more diffuse and penetrates tissues in the alveoli and the villi. Lymphoid tissue contains both lymphocytes and phagocytes. Lymphocytes are produced from stem cells in the **primary** organs and then migrate to the **secondary** organs such as the spleen when they are mature and ready to initiate specific defences against pathogens.

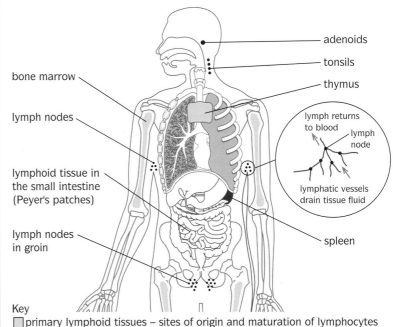

Key
☐ primary lymphoid tissues – sites of origin and maturation of lymphocytes
• secondary lymphoid tissues – sites where mature lymphocytes migrate

● *Figure 6.1* The lymphoid system.

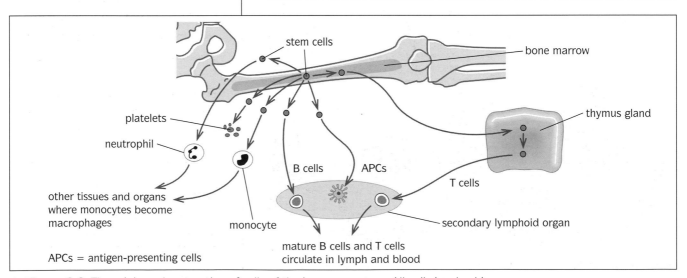

● *Figure 6.2* The origin and maturation of cells of the immune system. All cells involved in defence originate from stem cells in bone marrow. Red blood cells and platelets originate from the same place. T cells migrate to the thymus gland to mature.

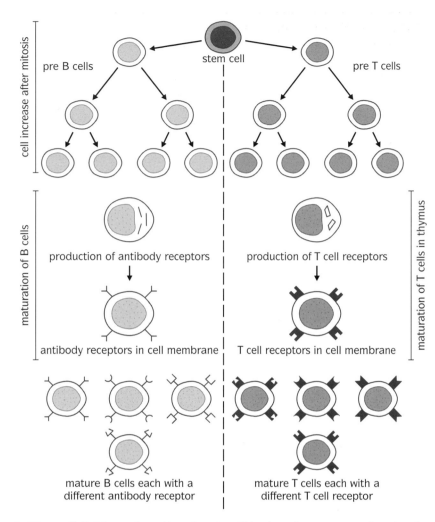

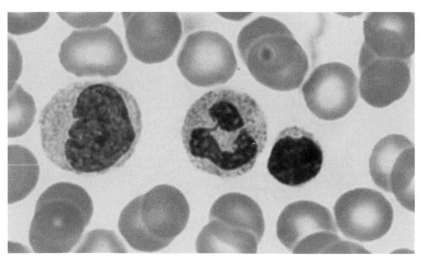

● **Figure 6.3** Maturation of lymphocytes. This gives rise to a great diversity of B and T cells and happens before any foreign antigens are encountered. T cells mature in the thymus. It is likely that B cells mature in bone marrow.

● **Figure 6.4** A monocyte (left), a neutrophil (centre) and a lymphocyte (right) together with red blood cells in a blood smear which has been photographed through a light microscope. The cytoplasm of the neutrophil contains vacuoles full of hydrolytic enzymes (× 2200).

instead secrete **antibodies** and the hormone-like cytokines.

There are two groups of lymphocytes:

1 **T lymphocytes** (often called **T cells**);
2 **B lymphocytes** (often called **B cells**).

Both groups of cells go through a maturing process which starts just before birth *(figure 6.3)*. Lymphocytes must go through this process before they can take part in the specific response. During this maturation many different types of lymphocytes develop. This gives the specific immune system the ability to respond to any type of pathogen that enters the body. B cells probably mature in bone marrow before leaving to spread throughout the lymphoid system *(figures 6.1 and 6.2)*. Immature T cells migrate from bone marrow to mature in the thymus gland. This gland doubles in size between birth and puberty, but after puberty it shrinks. Many immature T cells (perhaps as many as 90%) do not leave the thymus as they are selectively destroyed *(figure 6.5)*.

SAQ 6.3 _____

Describe the differences between the neutrophil and the lymphocyte shown in *figure 6.4*.

SAQ 6.4 _____

Calculate the actual size of the neutrophil shown in *figure 6.4*.

Each B cell is genetically programmed to express just one type of specific receptor on its cell surface. These receptor molecules are similar to the regions of antibody molecules that combine specifically with antigens. During the maturation process antibody genes of each developing B cell rearrange to give one of as many as 10 million different possible variants. These code for the different antibodies and cell surface proteins. For every antigen that enters the body, there will be some mature B cells with receptors that will recognise it. Some B cell receptors fit better with a particular antigen than others: they have a higher affinity and the cells will produce antibody molecules that will be very effective. When B cells are activated during an infection large numbers of different types respond, each type making a different antibody. This improves the overall defence against the pathogen. Some B cells make antibodies which bind to the body's own proteins. It is likely that most of these B cells are killed in the bone marrow before they are released and start to do any harm.

T cells mature in a different way *(figure 6.5)*. While in the thymus, differentiating T cells express specific surface receptors called **T cell receptors**. These only recognise antigens when they are present in the groove of a group of membrane proteins known as MHC proteins. MHC stands for major histocompatibility complex. Cells in the thymus with MHC proteins present the body's own antigens to developing T cells. Any T cells that bind strongly to these MHC–antigen complexes are killed. If these T cells were not killed they would direct an attack against the body's own cells and tissues. Some T cells which bind less well to these 'self' antigens survive, but are inactivated after they are released from the thymus. Sometimes this inactivation goes wrong and the immune system attacks the body's own

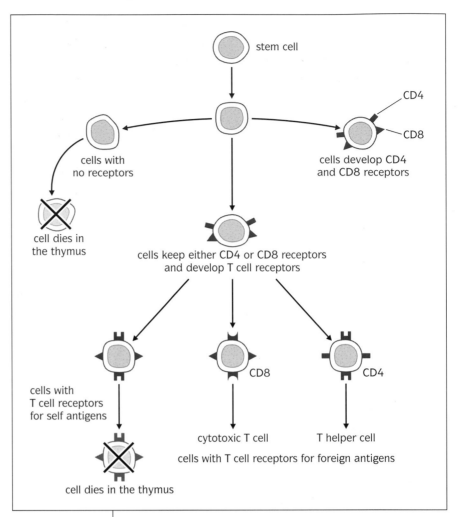

● *Figure 6.5* T cell maturation in the thymus.

cells causing an auto-immune disease such as rheumatoid arthritis. Most of the T cells that survive the maturation process in the thymus are those that recognise foreign antigens. Many millions of different T cell types are produced and released from the thymus, but there are only small numbers of cells with each type of receptor.

T cells develop another group of glycoprotein receptors known as **CD receptors**, which identify the sub-group to which each T cell belongs. **T helper cells** (T_h) have CD4 receptors, and cytotoxic T cells (T_c) have CD8. T cells play a central role in controlling the specific immune system and the CD receptors stabilise the binding of T cell receptors to MHC proteins on the surfaces of host cells, helping in the identification of foreign antigens. Any maturing T cells that do not develop CD receptors are killed in the thymus.

When mature, both B and T cells circulate between the blood and the lymph. This ensures that they are distributed throughout the body so that they come into contact with pathogens and with each other. They concentrate in the lymph nodes and in organs such as the spleen.

SAQ 6.5

Suggest why the thymus gland becomes smaller after puberty.

Defence against bacteria

The immune system's defences against bacteria and viruses are slightly different. This is because most bacteria grow and divide outside the cells of infected tissues. Viruses invade cells and multiply inside them. In both cases the non-specific system is the first line of defence. The central feature of this response to infection by bacteria is inflammation (*figure 6.6*). When bacteria enter through a wound in skin or a mucous membrane, mast cells in the underlying tissue release histamine to stimulate the movement of phagocytes and plasma proteins from the blood. The tissue becomes hot, red and swollen.

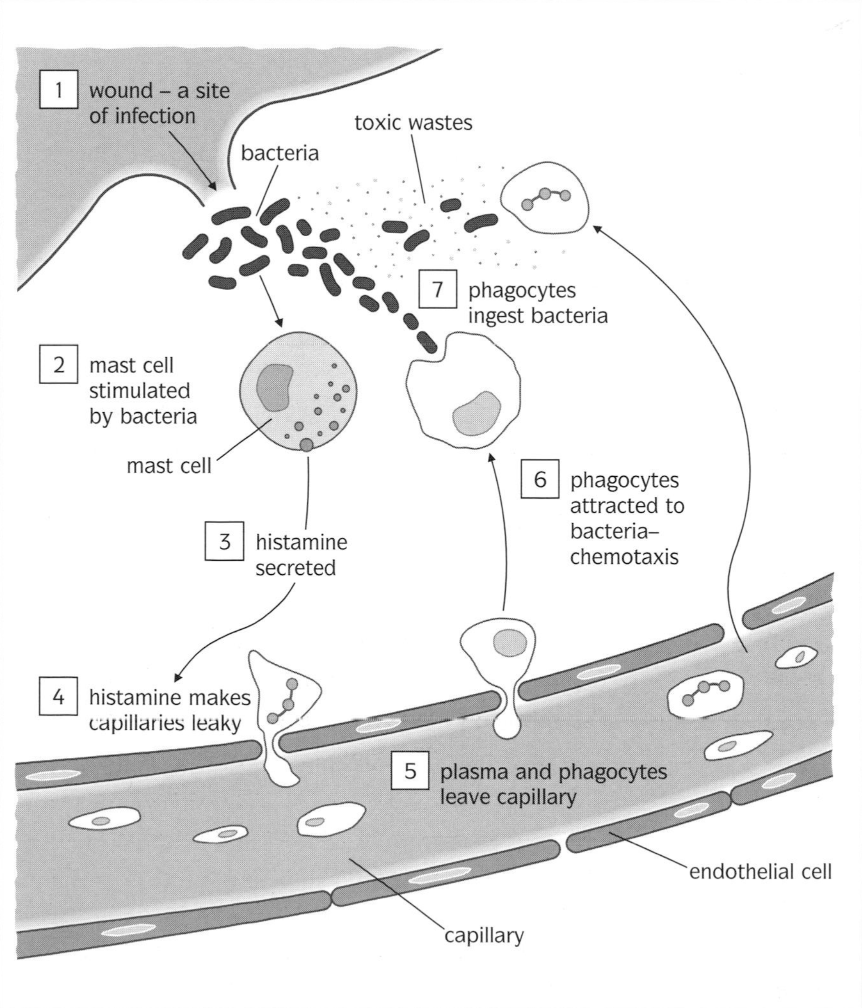

Phagocytosis

During the early part of an infection, neutrophils collect at a site of infection. They are attracted by chemicals released by bacteria and substances released by host cells such as histamine from mast cells. Plasma proteins known as **complement** are also activated by invading bacteria and help to attract neutrophils. This movement of phagocytes towards a site of infection is called **chemotaxis**. Receptor proteins on neutrophil cell surface membranes bind to surface compounds on the bacteria (*figure 6.7*). This adherence stimulates the neutrophil surface membrane to infold, surrounding the bacteria in a **phagosome** (*figure 6.8*). Often adherence occurs after bacteria are 'labelled' by complement and/or by antibodies. Lysosomes fuse with phagosomes to form phagolysosomes in which bacteria are killed by highly toxic free radicals (e.g. nitric oxide, $NO^{\cdot}$, and superoxide, $O_2^{\cdot-}$) and hydrogen peroxide (H_2O_2). Bacterial cell walls are digested by lysozyme, an enzyme which hydrolyses the glycosidic bonds between sugars in the polysaccharide walls of bacteria. Proteases, nucleases and other enzymes digest the rest of the cell. The products of digestion are absorbed into the cytoplasm. Neutrophils have a short life and after killing and digesting some bacteria they die. Dead neutrophils often collect at a site of infection to form **pus**.

● *Figure 6.6* Inflammation in response to bacterial infection.

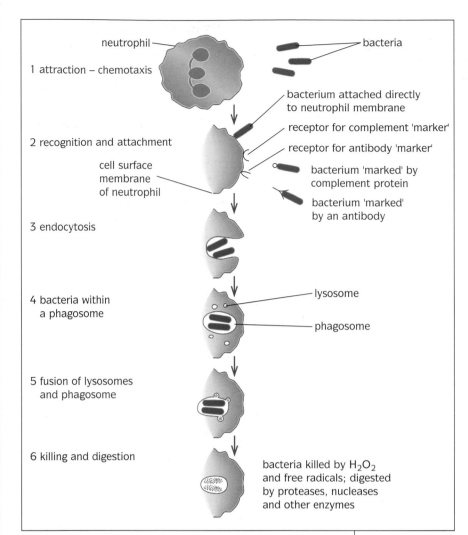

● *Figure 6.7* The stages of phagocytosis.

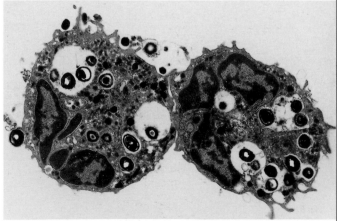

● *Figure 6.8* A transmission electron micrograph of two neutrophils that have ingested several *Staphylococcus* bacteria. Notice at the extreme left one bacterium being engulfed. Compare this photograph with *figure 6.7* and find the lobed nuclei and phagosomes. (× 6500)

On their own, neutrophils are not very successful at removing bacteria. They require the help of the specific immune system.

Specific immunity

The specific immune system improves and enhances the activity of the non-specific system. An **immune response** is a response to a specific pathogen and results in the production of a range of cellular and chemical agents of defence directed at that pathogen.

During the initial infection some bacteria circulate around the body and reach the lymph nodes and spleen where they are ingested by macrophages. These do not degrade the bacteria completely, but cut up the surface molecules from the bacterial cell walls and cell membranes. These pieces act as antigens and the macrophages display them on their cell surface membranes in grooves within MHC proteins. This process is called **antigen presentation** and the cells that do this, such as macrophages, are called **antigen-presenting cells (APCs).**

Inside lymph nodes APCs join with T helper (T$_h$) cells and B cells *(figure 6.9)*. An APC displaying a specific antigen will make contact with T$_h$ cells that have T cell receptors complementary in shape to that antigen. At the beginning of an infection there is a very small number of T$_h$ cells with appropriate receptors. When these are activated by APCs they divide by mitosis to form a clone. The clone of T$_h$ cells secrete cytokines to activate B cells nearby which also have surface receptors complementary in shape to the antigen. These B cells also divide to form clones.

So during antigen presentation, APCs *select* the T and B cells which have membrane receptors that are complementary in shape to the antigens that

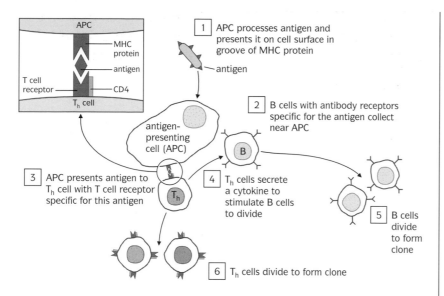

1   APC processes antigen and presents it on cell surface in groove of MHC protein

antigen

antigen-presenting cell (APC)

2   B cells with antibody receptors specific for the antigen collect near APC

3   APC presents antigen to T$_h$ cell with T cell receptor specific for this antigen

4   T$_h$ cells secrete a cytokine to stimulate B cells to divide

5   B cells divide to form clone

6   T$_h$ cells divide to form clone

● **Figure 6.9** Antigen presentation and activation of T and B cells. Antigen-presenting cells (APCs) expose bacterial antigen on their cell surface membranes. Only those T$_h$ cells which have a receptor complementary in shape to the antigen will be activated by the APC. T$_h$ cell receptors only recognise antigens when they are in the grooves of MHC proteins.

they have exposed. This is known as **clonal selection** *(figure 6.10)*. As bacteria have many surface antigens, APCs will activate many different T and B cell clones to give a **polyclonal** response to the infection. **Clonal expansion** by mitosis is necessary to produce large numbers of lymphocytes with the ability to destroy the pathogen. Clonal selection and expansion are illustrated in *figure 6.10*.

SAQ 6.6

a   Describe what happens during antigen presentation.

b   Explain why only some T and B cells respond during antigen presentation.

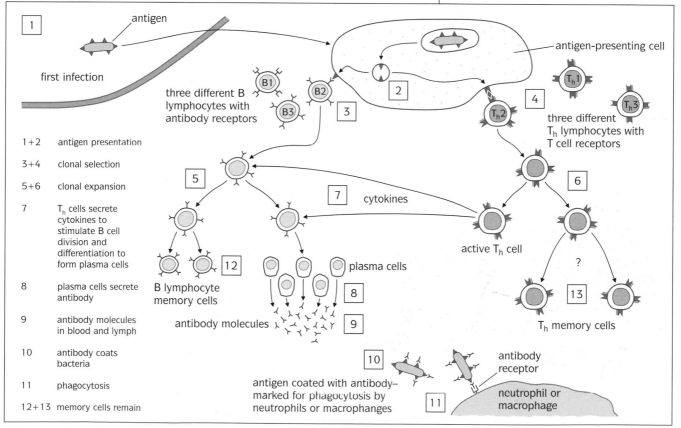

first infection

antigen

antigen-presenting cell

three different B lymphocytes with antibody receptors

three different T$_h$ lymphocytes with T cell receptors

cytokines

active T$_h$ cell

B lymphocyte memory cells

plasma cells

antibody molecules

T$_h$ memory cells

antigen coated with antibody– marked for phagocytosis by neutrophils or macrophanges

antibody receptor

neutrophil or macrophage

1+2   antigen presentation

3+4   clonal selection

5+6   clonal expansion

7   T$_h$ cells secrete cytokines to stimulate B cell division and differentiation to form plasma cells

8   plasma cells secrete antibody

9   antibody molecules in blood and lymph

10   antibody coats bacteria

11   phagocytosis

12+13   memory cells remain

● **Figure 6.10** Clonal selection and clonal expansion. Clones T$_h$-2 and B-2 have the specific receptor for the antigen presented by the APC. Only these clones are selected by the APC. Activated cells divide following mitosis to form large numbers of cells – this is clonal expansion. Activated B cells are plasma cells. The clones of B cells form memory cells. T memory cells may also exist.

SAQ 6.7

Explain the terms *clonal selection* and *clonal expansion*.

Humoral and cell-mediated immunity

Some pathogens, such as various bacteria, occupy spaces within the body and do not enter our cells. **Humoral immunity** is the action of antibodies released into the blood and lymph to act against these pathogens. ('Humoral' comes from a mediaeval word referring to body fluids.) Other pathogens enter cells and are much more difficult to remove. Antibodies are of limited use because they cannot cross the cell surface membranes to reach the pathogens inside. Cytotoxic T cells and macrophages remove these pathogens by destroying infected host cells. This is **cell-mediated immunity**, in which cells of the immune system directly kill pathogens, unlike the case of humoral immunity, in which antibodies work at a distance from the plasma cells that secrete them.

Humoral response

Activated B cells divide into plasma cells *(figures 6.10 and 6.11)*. Plasma cells produce antibody molecules very quickly, up to several thousand

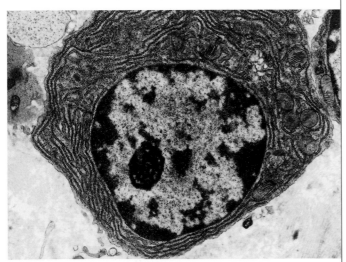

● *Figure 6.11* A plasma cell. The rough endoplasmic reticulum is filled with antibody molecules. Notice the Golgi body for combining the polypeptides that make up antibody molecules and then packaging them in vacuoles. Plasma cells secrete antibodies into blood or lymph by exocytosis. (× 25 000)

molecules a second. They secrete antibodies into the blood, lymph or onto the surfaces of mucous membranes, such as those in the lungs and the gut. Plasma cells are short-lived: after several weeks, their numbers decrease but the antibody molecules they have secreted remain in the blood for some time. Eventually, however, the concentration of antibodies decreases too.

Cell-mediated response

The cell-mediated response involves T cells and macrophages. The response of T cells to infection is different to that shown by B cells. By secreting cytokines, T_h cells activate macrophages and T_c cells to kill the pathogens that invade cells, such as viruses, some fungi, *Plasmodium* and *Mycobacterium*. The way in which cell-mediated immunity defends us against viruses is described below.

Defence against viruses

Viruses invade host cells and direct them to manufacture new virus particles. Unlike most bacteria, which invade tissues but remain outside cells, viruses circulate in the body fluids for only a fairly short time. Soon after cells are invaded by viruses, the cell surface membranes begin to express, or display, viral proteins that announce the fact that these cells are infected. These viral antigens stimulate clonal selection and clonal expansion of T and B cells in just the same way as bacterial antigens, but the antibodies secreted by B cells are only effective for a short time, because viruses are not in the blood for long. T_h cells stimulate T_c cells with receptors specific to the antigens of the invading virus to divide and form clones. These T_c clones patrol the body searching cell surfaces for the viral antigens. They then attack these infected cells by injecting toxic chemicals to destroy them and any virus particles inside *(figure 6.12)*. In addition, T cells and other cells including macrophages secrete the cytokine interferon, which inhibits viral replication in infected cells and prevents the spread of viruses to other cells.

The humoral and cell-mediated responses are activated by T_h cells. If immune responses were left

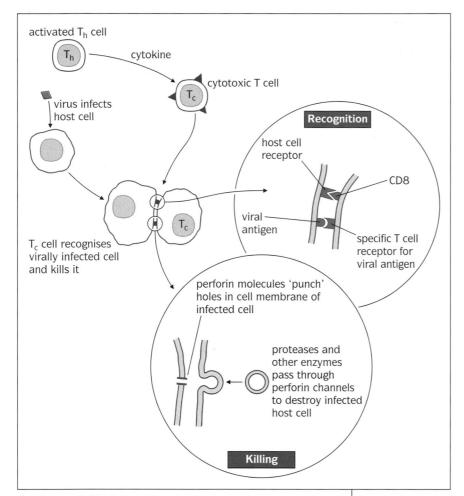

activated T$_h$ cell

cytokine

cytotoxic T cell

virus infects host cell

T$_c$ cell recognises virally infected cell and kills it

Recognition

host cell receptor

CD8

viral antigen

specific T cell receptor for viral antigen

perforin molecules 'punch' holes in cell membrane of infected cell

proteases and other enzymes pass through perforin channels to destroy infected host cell

Killing

● *Figure 6.12* Cell-mediated response – defence against a virus attack. APCs present viral antigens released from infected cells to a specific T$_h$ cell with the appropriate receptor. This T$_h$ cell activates T$_c$ cells, which search out and destroy host cells that are infected with the same virus.

to these cells alone, then they could go out of control. A variety of cellular and molecular mechanisms 'switch off' or suppress immune responses so that they only last until the pathogen is removed. This may be the responsibility of separate T suppressor cells which secrete cytokines to suppress lymphocyte activity. Although this process is not fully understood, both cells with CD4 receptors and ones with CD8 receptors have been found with the ability to act as T suppressor cells.

SAQ 6.8

Explain the difference between humoral and cell-mediated immunity.

SAQ 6.9

Suggest what would happen if T$_h$ cells were absent or inhibited during an immune response.

Antibodies and long-term immunity

Antibodies are globular glyco-proteins forming the group of plasma proteins called **immunoglobulins**. The basic antibody molecule consists of four polypeptide chains, two long or heavy chains and two short or light chains (*figures 6.13* and *6.14*). The chains are held together by disulphide bridges. Each molecule has two identical antigen binding sites, which are formed by both light and heavy chains. The sequences of amino acids in these regions make a specific three dimensional shape which binds to one antigen. This is the variable region of the antibody and is specific to each type of antibody produced. The hinge region gives the flexibility for the antibody molecule to bind around the antigen. Some antibodies act as labels to identify antigens as appropriate targets for phagocytes and complement proteins to destroy. Antitoxins are a special group of antibodies which neutralise the toxins released by bacteria such as those that cause diphtheria, tetanus and cholera (*figure 6.15*).

There are a number of different classes of antibody and they have different functions (*table 6.2* and *figure 6.15*). Even though they have different structures, they share common sub-units in their structure (*figures 6.13* and *6.14*). The variable regions show great diversity, but the constant regions of the heavy chains in each class are the same and carry out the same function. For example, the heavy chains of IgE bind to receptors on mast cells triggering them to release histamine and cause inflammation (*figure 6.6*).

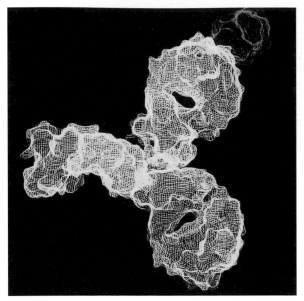

● **Figure 6.13** A model of an antibody made using computer graphics. The main part is the antibody molecule and the small part in the top right hand corner is an antigen bound to one of the two identical binding sites. Compare this with *figure 6.14*.

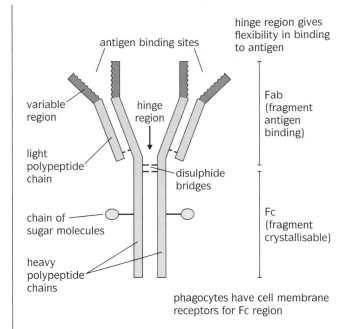

phagocytes have cell membrane receptors for Fc region

● **Figure 6.14** A diagram of an antibody molecule. Antigen–antibody binding occurs at the variable regions. An antigen fits into the binding site like a substrate fitting into the active site of an enzyme.

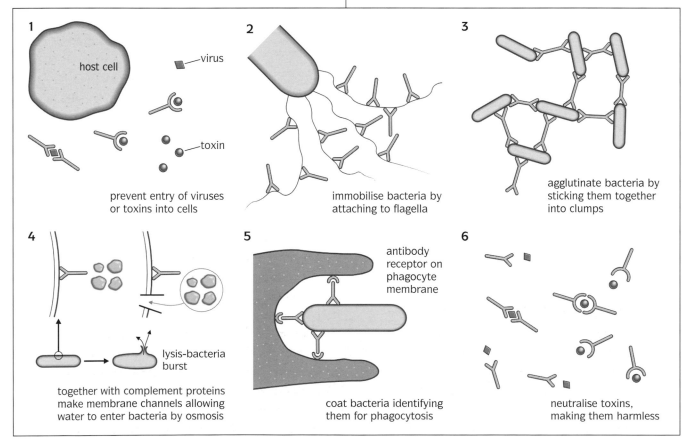

● **Figure 6.15** The functions of antibodies. Antibodies have different functions according to the type of antigen to which they bind.

Antibody class	Relative molecular mass	Number of antigen binding sites	Sites of action	Functions
Immunoglobulin G (IgG)	150 000	2	blood tissue fluid can cross placenta	• activates complement • enhances activity of macrophages • act as antitoxins • causes agglutination
Immunoglobulin M (IgM)	970 000	10	blood tissue fluid cannot cross placenta	• causes agglutination • activates complement
Immunoglobulin A (IgA)	160 000 or 320 000	2 or 4	saliva, tears bronchial secretions mucus secretions of small intestine prostate and vaginal secretions nasal fluid colostrum/breast milk	• inhibits bacteria adhering to host cells • prevents bacteria forming colonies on mucous membranes
Immunoglobulin E (IgE)	180 000	2	tissues	• heavy chains of IgE activate mast cells to release histamine • involved in response to infections by worms, and allergenic responses to harmless substances, e.g. pollen(hay fever)

● **Table 6.2** The four different classes of antibody and their functions. Whatever the class of antibody, each antibody molecule produced by a single clone of plasma cells possesses just one type of variable region and binds to one epitope (see *figure 6.16*).

Immunological memory

When an antigen is presented for the first time, clonal selection and clonal expansion both take some time. Once B cells have differentiated into plasma cells the specific antibodies that they secrete can be detected in the blood. The antibody secreted during this time is the large, IgM molecule (*table 6.2*). This **primary response** lasts several days or weeks and then the concentration of antibody decreases as the plasma cells stop secreting them. As the infection subsides, plasma cells die but memory B cells are left in the body.

If the antigen is reintroduced a few weeks later, there is a more rapid response with a higher concentration of antibody produced (*figure 6.17*). This **secondary response** occurs quickly because **memory cells** are formed during clonal expansion in the primary response (*figure 6.10*). Memory cells remain in the lymphoid system and circulate in blood and lymph constantly searching for the return of pathogens bearing the same antigen. On finding some, they divide rapidly to produce plasma cells. Memory T cells may also persist in the body, but the evidence for this is controversial.

Box 6B Antigens and epitopes

Antigens are macromolecules such as proteins, glyco-proteins and polysaccharides, which have many small areas made up of just a few amino acids or sugar molecules with specific shapes *(figure 6.16)*. These small areas are the antigenic determinants or **epitopes** that APCs present to B and T cells. Bacteria have many different surface antigens, each with many epitopes. This gives plenty of different binding sites for antibodies. Viruses are smaller, with few antigens on their surface and thus fewer sites to which antibodies can bind.

Only the T or B cells with the appropriate surface receptors will form a temporary complex with an APC presenting an epitope *(figure 6.9)*. One APC may present many different epitopes over its surface during an infection and so may activate many different clones of T and B cells. Each type of B cell expresses a slightly different antibody molecule on its surface membrane as a receptor. When activated by an APC and a T_h cell, specific B cells divide to form a clone of plasma cells that secrete many copies of the same antibody. Each plasma cell makes only one type of heavy chain and one type of light chain, so when the chains are assembled the antibody molecules made by a plasma cell only have one type of variable region. The variable regions on the light and heavy polypeptide chains have a unique shape determined by the sequence of amino acids. The shape of the variable region determines the type of epitope to which it binds.

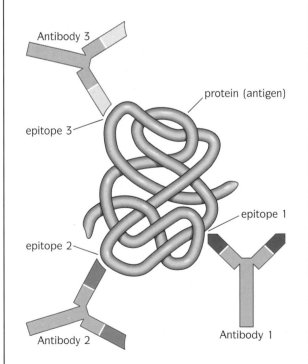

● *Figure 6.16* A protein antigen with small areas (epitopes) over its surface to which antibodies bind.

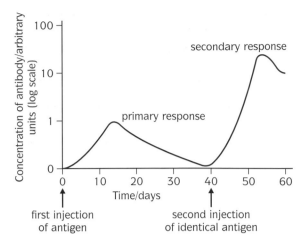

● *Figure 6.17* The changes in antibody concentration in the blood during a primary and secondary response to the same antigen.

The process is repeated each time the same antigen is identified. The secondary response is faster because there are many memory cells, which go through fewer divisions before differentiating into plasma cells. During the second exposure to an antigen more memory cells are produced so that the response to any further infections is just as or even more rapid. During the secondary response and any subsequent responses, more IgG is secreted than IgM.

Memory cells are the basis of immunological memory; they last for many years, often a lifetime. It is thought that APCs retain and continually expose antigens to memory cells, even when there is no infection, so that the memory is not lost. We suffer repeated infections of the common cold or influenza because there are many different strains of the viruses causing these diseases, each one expressing different antigens. Each time we have an infection with a different pathogen, antigen presentation, clonal selection and clonal expansion must occur before immunity is gained.

SAQ 6.10

There is only one strain of the chickenpox virus. Use the information in *figure 6.17* to explain:

a why we rarely catch chickenpox twice.

b why an exposure to chickenpox does not also provide immunity to measles.

SAQ 6.11

There are many different strains of the rhinovirus, which causes the common cold. Explain why people can catch several different colds in the space of a few months.

Active and passive immunity

The type of specific immunity described so far occurs during the course of an infection. This form of immunity is **active** because lymphocytes are activated by antigens on the surface of pathogens that have invaded the body. As this activation occurs naturally during an infection it is called **natural active immunity**. The immune response can also be activated artificially by injecting antigens into the body. This is the basis of **artificial active immunity**, more commonly known as **vaccination**. The immune response is similar to that following an infection, and the effect is the same – long-term immunity. In both natural and artificial active immunity antibody concentrations in the blood follow patterns similar to those shown in *figure 6.17*.

The main problem with both forms of active immunity is that it takes time for sufficient B and T cells to be produced to give an effective defence. During this time the infection may spread and the development of disease can be fatal. People who have a wound and are thought to be at risk of contracting the bacterial disease tetanus are given an injection of antitoxin. This is a preparation of human antibodies against the tetanus toxin. The antibodies are collected from blood donors who have recently been vaccinated against tetanus. Tetanus kills quickly: before the body's natural primary response can take place. But antitoxin provides immediate protec-tion. However, this protection is only temporary as the antibodies are not produced by the body's own B cells and are therefore regarded as foreign. They are removed from the circulation by phagocytes in the liver and spleen.

This type of immunity to tetanus is **passive immunity** because the B and T cells have not been activated and plasma cells have not produced any antibody. More specifically, it is **artificial passive immunity**: the antibodies have come from another person who has encountered the antigen.

The immune system of a newborn infant is not as effective as that of a child or an adult. Maternal antibodies cross the placenta during pregnancy and remain in the infant for several months *(figure 6.18)*. For example, antibodies against measles may last for four months or more in the infant's blood. **Colostrum**, the thick yellowish fluid produced by a mother's breasts for the first four or five days after birth, is rich in IgA, which remains on the surface of an infant's gut wall and passes through into the blood undi-gested. IgA acts in the gut to prevent the growth of bacteria and viruses and also circulates in the blood. This is **natural passive immunity**. The features of active and passive immunity are compared in *table 6.3*.

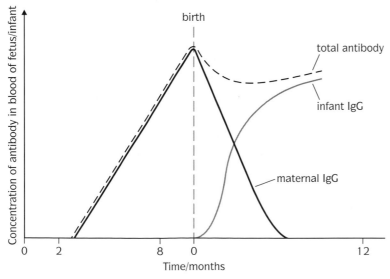

● *Figure 6.18* The concentrations of antibody in the blood of a fetus and an infant.

SAQ 6.12

Explain the difference between artificial active immunisation (vaccination) and artificial passive immunisation.

Feature	Active	Passive
antigen encountered	yes	no
immune response	yes	no
clonal selection	yes	no
clonal expansion	yes	no
time before antibodies appear in blood	several weeks during primary response	immediate
production of memory cells	yes	no
protection	permanent	temporary

● **Table 6.3** Active and passive immunity

SAQ 6.13

Explain the pattern of maternal and infant IgG shown in *figure 6.18*.

SAQ 6.14

Explain the advantages of natural passive immunity for newborn infants.

Vaccination

A **vaccine** is a preparation containing antigenic material, which may be a whole live microorganism, a dead one, a harmless version (known as an *attenuated organism*), a harmless form of a toxin (toxoid) or a preparation of surface antigens. They are either given by injection into a vein or muscle, or are taken orally.

Immunity derived from a natural infection is often so good at providing protection because the immune system has met living organisms which persist inside the body for some time, so that the specific immune system has time to develop an effective response. When possible, vaccination tries to mimic this. Sometimes this works very well, when vaccines contain live microorganisms. The microorganisms reproduce, albeit rather slowly, so that the immune system is continually presented with a large dose of antigens. APCs are far more effective if they have complete, living bacteria or viruses to deal with. Less effective are those vaccines that do not mimic an infection because they are made from dead bacteria or viruses. Proteins from dead viruses do not get presented by APCs to activate T_c cells.

Some vaccines are highly effective and one injection may well give a lifetime's protection. Less effective ones need booster injections to stimulate secondary responses that give enhanced protection (*figure 6.17*). It is often a good idea to receive booster injections if you are likely to be exposed to a disease, even though you may have been vaccinated as a child.

Problems with vaccines

Poor response

Some people do not respond at all, or not very well, to vaccinations. This may be because they have a defective immune system and as a result do not develop the necessary B and T cell clones. It may also be because they suffer from malnutrition, particularly protein energy malnutrition, and do not have enough protein to make antibodies or clones of lymphocytes. These people are at a high risk of developing infectious diseases and transmitting them to people who have no immunity. People vaccinated with a live virus may pass it out in their faeces during the primary response and may infect others. This is why it is better to vaccinate a large number of people at the same time to give **herd immunity**, or to ensure that all children are vaccinated within a few months of birth. Herd immunity interrupts transmission in a population, so that those who are susceptible never encounter the infectious agents concerned.

SAQ 6.15

Explain why malnourished children give very weak responses to vaccines.

Antigenic variation

In spite of years of research, there are no vaccines for the common cold. The type of rhinovirus that causes most colds has 113 different strains. It may be impossible to develop a vaccine that protects against all of these.

The influenza virus mutates regularly to give different antigens. When there are minor changes in the epitopes of the viral coat proteins, memory cells will still recognise them and start a secondary response. These minor changes are called **antigenic drift**. More serious are major changes in epitope structure – known as **antigenic shift** – when influenza viruses change their antigens considerably and the protective immunity given by vaccination against the first strain is ineffective against the second. The World Health Organisation (WHO) recommends the type of vaccine to use according to the antigens that are common at the time. The vaccine is changed every year.

There are, as yet, no effective vaccines against the diseases which are caused by protoctists such as malaria and sleeping sickness. This is because these pathogens are eukaryotes with many more genes than bacteria and viruses. They express many hundreds, or even thousands, of antigens on their cell surfaces. *Plasmodium* passes through three stages in its life cycle while it is in the human host. Each stage has its own specific antigens. This means that effective vaccines would have to contain antigens to all three stages or be specific to the infective stage. The latter would only work if the immune system can give an effective response in the short period of time (a few hours) between the mosquito bite and the infection of liver cells (*figure 5.3*). *Trypanosoma*, the causative agent of sleeping sickness, has a total of about a thousand different antigens and changes them every four or five days. This makes it impossible for the immune system to respond effectively and after several weeks the body is completely overwhelmed by the parasite, with fatal consequences.

SAQ. 6.16

Explain why humans cannot produce an effective immune response to an infection by *Trypanosoma*.

Antigenic concealment

Some pathogens evade attack by the immune system by living inside cells. For example when *Plasmodium* enters liver cells or red blood cells, it is protected against the humoral immune system. Some parasitic worms conceal themselves by covering their bodies in host antigens, so they remain invisible to the immune system. Other pathogens suppress the immune system by parasitising cells such as macrophages and T cells. It is very difficult to develop effective vaccines against these pathogens because there is such a short period of time for an immune response to occur before the pathogen 'hides'.

Another example is *Vibrio cholerae* (the causative agent of cholera), which remains in the intestine where it is beyond the reach of many antibodies. The cholera vaccine is injected rather than taken orally and so it does not stimulate antibody production in the intestine. Neither does it stimulate the production of an antitoxin against choleragen. An oral vaccine against cholera is currently being developed.

SAQ. 6.17

Name one pathogen that parasitises **a** macrophages and **b** T helper cells.

The eradication of smallpox

Smallpox was an acute, highly infectious disease caused by the variola virus and transmitted by direct contact. It was a terrible disease. Red spots containing a transparent fluid would appear all over the body (*figure 6.19*). These then filled with thick pus. Eyelids became swollen and could become glued together. Sufferers often had to be prevented from tearing at their flesh. Many people who recovered were permanently blind and disfigured by scabs left when the pustules dried out. Smallpox killed between 12 and 30% of its victims.

The World Health Organisation started an eradication programme in 1956; in 1967 it stated its intention to rid the world of the disease in ten years. There were two main aspects of the programme: vaccination and surveillance. Successful attempts were made across the world to vaccinate in excess of 80% of populations at risk of the disease. When a case of smallpox was reported, everyone in the household and the 30 surrounding households, as well as other relatives and possible contacts in the area, were vaccinated. This **ring vaccination** protected everyone who could possibly

● **Figure 6.19** A Bangladeshi child showing the characteristic pustules of smallpox. This photograph was taken in a refugee camp in India in 1973.

have come into contact with a person with the disease, reduced the chances of transmission and contained the disease. The last strongholds of smallpox remained in East Africa, Afghanistan and the Indian subcontinent. Eradication was most difficult in Ethiopia and Somalia, where many people lived in remote districts well away from main roads which were no more than dirt tracks. In the late 1970s the two countries went to war, and even though large parts of Ethiopia were overrun by the Somalis, the eradication programme continued. The last case of smallpox was reported in Somalia in 1977. The WHO finally declared the world free of smallpox in 1980.

The eradication programme was successful for a number of reasons.

■ The variola virus was stable; it did not mutate and change its surface antigens. This meant that the same vaccine could be used everywhere in the world throughout the campaign. It was therefore cheap to produce.

■ The vaccine was made from a harmless strain of a similar virus (vaccinia) and was effective because it was a 'live' vaccine.

■ The vaccine was freeze-dried and could be kept at high temperatures for as long as 6 months. This made it suitable for use in the tropics.

■ Infected people were easy to identify.

■ The vaccine was easy to administer and was even more effective after the development of a stainless steel, reusable needle for its delivery. This 'bifurcated needle' had two prongs, which were used to push the vaccine into the skin.

■ The smallpox virus did not linger in the body after an infection, then become active later to form a reservoir of infection.

■ The virus did not infect animals, which made it easier to break the transmission cycle.

■ Many 16- to 17-year-olds became enthusiastic vaccinators and suppliers of information about cases; this was especially valuable in remote areas.

The eradication of smallpox is a medical success story. It has been more difficult to repeat this success with other infectious diseases. This is partly because of the more unstable political situation in the late 1970s and 1980s particularly in Africa, Latin America and parts of Asia such as Afghanistan. Public health facilities are difficult to organise in developing countries with poor infrastructure, few trained personnel and limited financial resources. They are almost impossible to maintain during periods of civil unrest or during a war. Nevertheless, the WHO declared the Americas to be free of polio in 1991 and there are hopes to eliminate the disease completely by 2000 *(figure 6.20)*.

Measles

Measles is caused by a virus which is spread by airborne droplets. It causes a rash and fever. The disease rarely affects infants under eight months of age as they have passive immunity in the form of antibodies that have crossed the placenta from their mother. Measles used to be a common childhood disease in the UK and other developed countries, but is now quite rare because most children are vaccinated. However, epidemics do occur in the developed world, for example in the USA in 1989/90 when there were 55 000 cases and 132 deaths.

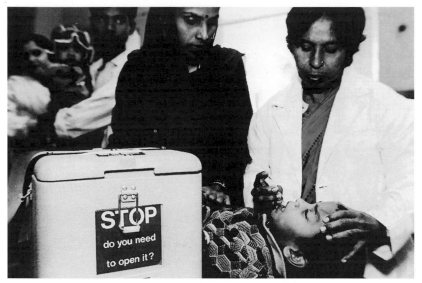

● *Figure 6.20* An Indian child receiving a vaccine against polio. Note the cold box for storage of the vaccine. India has 60% of all world cases of polio. On 9 December 1995 the Indian government organised a programme to vaccinate 80 million children under 3 years old. This was followed by another programme initiated on 2 January 1996.

Measles is a major disease in developing countries, particularly in cities where people live in overcrowded, insanitary conditions and where there is a high birth rate. The measles virus is transmitted easily in these conditions and it infects mainly malnourished infants suffering from vitamin A deficiency. Measles is responsible for many cases of childhood blindness and it also causes severe brain damage, which can be fatal. In 1993 it was estimated that there were over 45 million cases of measles and 1.16 million deaths making it the

ninth leading cause of death worldwide. Most of those who die from measles are young malnourished children who do not have the resistance to fight it.

Measles is a preventable disease and one that can be eradicated by a worldwide surveillance and vaccination programme. However, a programme of one-dose-vaccination has not eliminated the disease in any country despite high coverage of the population. This is explained by the poor response to the vaccine shown by some children who need several boosters to develop full immunity. In large cities with high birth rates and shifting populations, it can be difficult to give boosters, follow up cases of measles and trace contacts. Migrants and refugees often form reservoirs of infection. They start epidemics and spread the disease to surrounding rural areas. This makes measles a very difficult disease to eliminate even with high vaccination coverage.

Measles is highly infectious and it is estimated that herd immunity of 93 to 95% is required to prevent transmission in a population. As the currently available vaccine has a success rate of 95%, this means that the whole population needs to be vaccinated and infants must be vaccinated within about eight months of birth. Many countries achieve up to 80% or more coverage with measles vaccination *(figure 6.21)*, and it is hoped to declare the Americas free of the disease by 2000. With coverage of under 50% in Africa, it is likely that the disease will still persist there for many years to come.

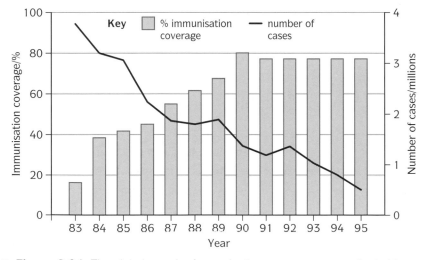

● *Figure 6.21* The global measles immunisation programme coordinated by the WHO has increased the immunisation coverage to about 80% of young children. As a result, the number of cases reported each year has decreased significantly.

Monoclonal antibodies

Most protein-based antigens have several or many different epitopes. When a protein-based antigen is injected into a laboratory animal it produces a polyclonal response, as many different clones of B cells respond and produce antibodies matching the different epitopes. It is difficult to extract these and purify them because the animal's blood contains many other antibodies in addition to those it has just produced in response to the injected antigen. It also requires collecting a large quantity of blood and purifying it. This is, however, how some specific antibodies used in passive immunisation are prepared.

A **monoclonal antibody** (often shortened to **monoclonal** or simply **mAb**) is a single pure antibody which combines with only one specific epitope. Monoclonal antibodies are produced by growing one clone of B cells in culture and collecting the antibodies that they release (see box 6C). Monoclonals are now used in just about every area of biomedical research, in many diagnostic tests and in treatment for some diseases. The great advantage of mAbs is their ability to identify and target specific sites such as cell surface marker proteins.

Monoclonals in diagnosis

Uses of monoclonal antibodies in diagnosis include:

■ blood typing for transfusions;

■ tissue typing for transplants;

Box 6C Making monoclonal antibodies

Monoclonal antibodies are obtained from single B cell clones. B cells do not grow in tissue culture, but this problem is solved by fusing them with malignant B cell tumour cells (myeloma cells) to make hybrid cells known as **hybridomas** *(figure 6.22)*. Myeloma cells are immortal: they continue growing and dividing in tissue culture, but they do not make any antibodies. Hybridoma cells too are capable of growing and dividing in tissue culture if they are given adequate nutrients; they also secrete antibodies.

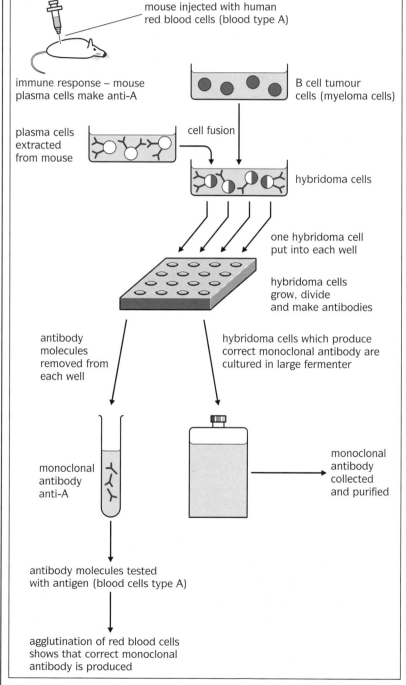

mouse injected with human red blood cells (blood type A)

immune response – mouse plasma cells make anti-A

B cell tumour cells (myeloma cells)

plasma cells extracted from mouse

cell fusion

hybridoma cells

one hybridoma cell put into each well

hybridoma cells grow, divide and make antibodies

antibody molecules removed from each well

hybridoma cells which produce correct monoclonal antibody are cultured in large fermenter

monoclonal antibody anti-A

monoclonal antibody collected and purified

antibody molecules tested with antigen (blood cells type A)

agglutination of red blood cells shows that correct monoclonal antibody is produced

● *Figure 6.22* Making monoclonal antibodies. Activated B cells are fused with myeloma cells, which are cancerous B cells. The hybrid cells secrete the antibody made by the activated B cell.

- identification of pathogens (e.g. gonorrhoea, *Chlamydia*, different types of the infective stage of *Plasmodium*);
- pregnancy testing;
- identification and location of cancers (e.g. of the colon, rectum and ovary);
- classification of T and B cell leukaemias;
- following the progression of HIV infection.

The great advantage of using monoclonals is that all the antibodies produced by one clone of B cells are identical. This means that they can identify macromolecules with a very high degree of specificity. Monoclonals are now available for routine diagnostic tests such as those that identify different strains of pathogens, for example *Chlamydia*, which causes non-specific urethritis, the most common sexually transmitted disease in the UK.

It is normally difficult to distinguish *Chlamydia* from the bacterium that causes gonorrhoea, as it is herpes virus 1, which causes both cold sores on lips and genital infections, from herpes virus 2, which causes genital infections. Monoclonals make these identifications much easier.

Monoclonals and blood groups

Blood transfusion is successful if donated blood is compatible with the blood of recipients; if blood is not matched carefully the recipient's immune system will treat the blood as foreign and start an immune response against it. However, red blood cells have few cell surface antigens and it is possible to transfuse blood between people who have the same blood group.

Blood collected by blood banks is routinely tested (or 'typed') for two blood group systems: the ABO and Rhesus systems. Both systems are determined by molecules found on the surfaces of red blood cells. In the ABO system there are two of these cell surface marker molecules or antigens, known as A and B. In the Rhesus system there is one, which is known as D. Three monoclonal antibodies are used in the test: anti-A, anti-B and anti-D. When each monoclonal is mixed with a sample of blood it will cause the red blood cells to agglutinate if they have the appropriate antigen. When they agglutinate, the cells form clumps which can be seen without the aid of a micro-

scope. If red blood cells only have cell surface antigen A, then the blood will agglutinate with mAb anti-A, but not with mAb anti-B. This identifies the blood as belonging to group A. If there is no agglutination with anti-A or anti-B, then the blood is type O. Blood that agglutinates with mAb anti-D is Rhesus positive; blood that does not is Rhesus negative.

SAQ 6.18

Draw a table to show the results that can be expected if the following blood groups are tested with mAbs anti-A, anti-B and anti-D:
AB Rhesus+, O Rhesus −, A Rhesus +, B Rhesus −.

SAQ 6.19

Explain why it is important to type blood before it is given in a transfusion.

Before an organ transplant can take place, cell surface antigens on the donated organ and on tissues in the recipient must be typed to find a close match, otherwise the recipient will be more likely to reject the donated organ. There are many different types of cell surface antigens on tissues in organs such as the heart, lungs and liver. It is much more difficult to obtain a match for organ transplants than it is when matching blood for transfusion. Monoclonals are used to identify the different antigens used in tissue typing.

Monoclonals and pregnancy testing

Very soon after conception, the hormone human chorionic gonadotrophin (HCG) is secreted. The concentrations in the blood are very high and it is excreted in the urine. Before the development of a monoclonal test for HCG, it took some time to confirm a pregnancy. Now pregnancy testing can be done at home in a few minutes. A home test kit contains a sampler which has monoclonal antibody molecules specific to HCG. When the sampler is moistened with urine, the antibody molecules begin to move. If HCG is present then the monoclonals bind to it and carry it up the sampler; this positive result is indicated by a coloured line appearing on the sampler (*figure 6.23*). The test is sensitive enough to give a positive result on the

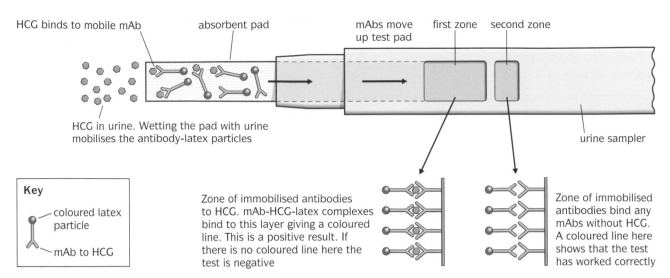

HCG binds to mobile mAb

absorbent pad

mAbs move up test pad

first zone

second zone

HCG in urine. Wetting the pad with urine mobilises the antibody-latex particles

urine sampler

Key

coloured latex particle

mAb to HCG

Zone of immobilised antibodies to HCG. mAb-HCG-latex complexes bind to this layer giving a coloured line. This is a positive result. If there is no coloured line here the test is negative

Zone of immobilised antibodies bind any mAbs without HCG. A coloured line here shows that the test has worked correctly

● *Figure 6.23* Pregnancy testing. The monoclonal antibody to HCG is bound to coloured latex particles.

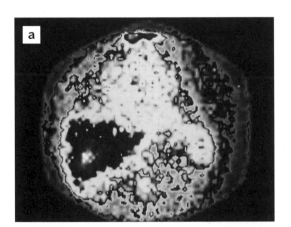

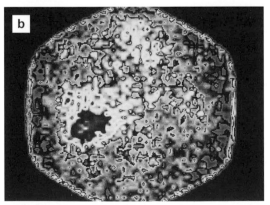

● *Figure 6.24* Immunoscintigrams. Monoclonals were made against ovarian cancer cells that had formed a secondary cancer in the liver. The monoclonals were labelled with a radio-isotope and injected into the blood. Radioactive emissions from the isotope are recorded by a camera that detects gamma radiation. (a) The triangular dark area shows where the monoclonals concentrated. (b) The same area after six weeks' treatment with chemotherapy.

first day of a missed period, which may be about fourteen days after conception.

Monoclonals and cancer

Tumour cells avoid destruction by T cells even though they often express surface antigens which are not found on other cells in the body. The presence of these antigens means that monoclonals can be made to identify them. Radioactive markers can be attached to the monoclonals specific to the antigens on tumour cells, so that the cells, which may be widely distributed in the body, can be found by scanning (*figure 6.24*).

SAQ 6.20

Explain why monoclonals are concentrated in one area in *figure 6.24*.

SUMMARY

■ The immune system consists of two parts: the non-specific system, which responds in the same way to repeated infections by any pathogen; and the specific system, which responds slowly during the first exposure to a pathogen, but much more quickly on future occasions.

■ Neutrophils and macrophages are phagocytes which destroy bacteria and viruses by killing and digesting them in phagosomes. This is phagocytosis.

- Phagocytes originate in the bone marrow and are produced there throughout life. Neutrophils circulate in the blood and enter tissues when inflammation occurs. Macrophages are more stationary inside tissues.

- Lymphocytes also originate in bone marrow, but migrate just before and after birth to other sites in the body.

- When B lymphocytes (B cells) are activated they form plasma cells, which secrete antibodies into body fluids: blood, tissue fluid and lymph. This is the humoral response. Antibodies act independently of the cells that secrete them.

- T lymphocytes (T cells) mature in the thymus and differentiate into two groups: T helper cells (T_h) and cytotoxic T cells (T_c). T_h cells activate B cells and T_c cells. T_c cells kill host cells infected with viruses, bacteria and parasites such as *Plasmodium*. Some T cells may act as the brakes of the immune system by becoming suppressor cells. The evidence for this is unclear.

- T cells do not secrete antibodies; the receptors in their cell surface membranes are similar to antibody molecules and these are used to identify specific antigens when they are activated at the beginning of an infection. T_h cells secrete cytokines to control the immune system.

- The killing of infected cells by T_c cells and macrophages is the cell-mediated response. This does not involve antibodies.

- Antigens are macromolecules such as proteins, glycoproteins and polysaccharides, which have many small areas made up of just a few amino acids or sugar molecules with specific shapes. These small areas are antigenic determinants, or epitopes. When antigens enter the body they stimulate the immune system to produce antibodies.

- Antibodies are globular glycoprotein molecules made by plasma cells. The simplest type of antibody (IgG) is made of two identical heavy polypeptides and two identical light polypeptides. The variable regions of the heavy and light polypeptides have specific shapes, so each type of antibody interacts with one specific epitope. Each molecule of IgG can bind to two antigens. Larger antibodies (IgM and IgA) have more than two antigen binding sites.

- Antibodies agglutinate bacteria; prevent viruses infecting cells; coat bacteria and viruses, so facilitating ingestion by phagocytes; act with plasma proteins to lyse bacteria; neutralise toxins.

- During an immune response, memory cells are formed which retain the ability to divide rapidly and differentiate into plasma cells or active T cells on a second exposure to the same antigen. This is the basis of immunological memory.

- Active immunity is the production of antibodies and active T cells during a primary immune response to an antigen that has been acquired naturally by infection or artificially by vaccination. This gives permanent immunity.

- Passive immunity is the introduction of antibodies from another source (human or animal). They can be acquired naturally across the placenta or in breast milk, or artificially when injected to provide immediate protection against dangerous diseases such as tetanus.

- The antigens used in vaccination may be a whole living organism, a dead one, a harmless version of a toxin (toxoid) or a preparation of surface antigens.

- It is difficult to develop successful vaccines against diseases for several reasons. Some pathogens have many different strains or can express different antigens during their life cycle within humans (antigenic variation). The causative organism of cholera remains in the intestine beyond the reach of the immune system. *Plasmodium* exposes many different antigens and remains within red blood cells and liver cells for much of its life cycle. *Mycobacterium* and HIV also parasitise host cells and cannot be reached by antibodies (antigenic concealment).

- Smallpox was eradicated by a programme of surveillance, contact tracing and 'ring' vaccination. It was made possible by the use of an effective 'live' vaccine. As there was only one strain of the smallpox virus only one vaccine was needed.

- Measles is a common disease of infants in impoverished areas of developing countries, especially in overcrowded cities. It is difficult to achieve a wide coverage of vaccination and malnourished children do not respond well to one dose of the vaccine.

- A monoclonal antibody is an antibody specific to one epitope. Monoclonals are used in blood typing, tissue typing, pregnancy testing kits, detecting cancerous tumours and other diagnoses.

Questions

1 Explain the difference between the following pairs of terms: **a** *active* and *passive immunity*, **b** *specific* and *non-specific immune systems*, **c** *clonal selection* and *clonal expansion*.

2 Discuss the roles of phagocytes and lymphocytes in defence against bacterial pathogens.

3 Explain how a new vaccine might be tested before becoming generally available.

4 Explain why measles is a major infectious disease in many developing countries.

5 Explain why vaccination has eliminated smallpox, but not malaria, measles, cholera or TB.

6 Discuss the roles of monoclonal antibodies in diagnosis.

Chapter seven

Drugs

By the end of this chapter you should be able to:

1 discuss the meaning of the term *drug*;

2 discuss the difference between socially acceptable and illicit drugs;

3 discuss the effects of heroin on the nervous system and on behaviour;

4 explain the meaning of the term *drug tolerance*, with reference to nicotine, alcohol and heroin;

5 distinguish between psychological and physical dependence;

6 describe the immediate and long-term consequences of alcohol consumption on the brain, peripheral nervous system and the liver;

7 discuss the social consequences of excessive alcohol use with particular reference to drinking and driving, aggressive behaviour, intra-family violence, family breakdown and petty crime.

What are drugs?

The term **drug** is difficult to define satisfactorily. In the widest sense drugs are chemical substances taken into the body or applied to the skin. This encompasses a very wide variety of substances, including nutrients such as vitamins and minerals, even water. It is more common to use the term to refer to substances which interfere with some aspect of metabolism. These drugs are taken to alter the progress of a disease and they interact with our metabolism or that of a pathogen, such as a bacterium. This definition would include medicines such as pain-killers and antibiotics. In an even more restricted sense, drugs are chemicals which interfere with the nervous system and cause changes in mental state and behaviour. These are **psychoactive drugs,** such as LSD, cannabis, alcohol, nicotine and heroin. It is drugs of this type which are dealt with in this chapter.

Socially acceptable and illicit drugs

Some drugs are widely accepted in all societies because of their medical importance. In the UK pain-killers, such as aspirin and paracetamol, are widely available 'over-the-counter' drugs; others, such as antibiotics, are available on prescription. Anaesthetics are used in hospitals and clinics.

Other drugs have important medical uses, but have become popular drugs of misuse because of their psychoactive effects. **Heroin** is such a drug. Amphetamines, which were widely prescribed in the past as appetite suppressants, remain popular drugs of misuse. Alcohol is used as a disinfectant and when drunk in moderation has few adverse effects on the body. In fact it has been shown to be beneficial in reducing the risk of heart disease. But in larger quantities alcohol increases the risks of cancer, depression, liver disease and brain damage. It is the world's favourite mood-altering drug, so it is hardly surprising that it is widely misused in many societies.

Cultural attitudes determine whether a drug is socially acceptable or not and make it difficult to distinguish between accepted use and misuse. Both alcohol and cannabis are intoxicants. The latter is considered by some to be no more harmful than the former. It is widely used among certain groups and it has been shown to relieve the symptoms of degenerative diseases. However, whereas in many countries alcohol is legal, the sale and possession of cannabis are not. The illegal drugs are those categorised in the Misuse of Drugs Act (1971). Legislation like this is the best indicator of the drugs that society considers unacceptable.

Attitudes to drugs change. Smoking was once considered very fashionable – even Oscar Wilde's Lady Bracknell approved. In the 1950s over half the population of the UK smoked. Since the health risks associated with smoking have been identified (see chapter 4), the percentage of the population who smoke has decreased and now it is less than 30%. Although the sale of tobacco products is licensed, smoking is still legal, but becoming less socially acceptable. Alcohol and tobacco are more widely accepted in certain societies, occupations, and social and ethnic groups than others. In some societies and ethnic groups the consumption of alcohol is illegal, for example it is proscribed by Islam.

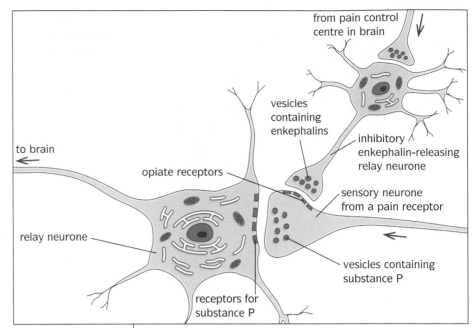

● *Figure 7.1* Synapses between a sensory, relay and inhibitory relay neurone in the grey matter of the spinal cord, showing the site of action of enkephalins. A pain receptor stimulates the sensory neurone, which forms a synapse with the relay neurone. The relay neurone transmits the pain information to a sensory centre in the brain. Enkephalins are released by the inhibitory relay neurone. They probably act by preventing the sensory neurone from triggering an impulse in the relay neurone. Substance P is the neurotransmitter between the two.

SAQ 7.1

Explain how you might tell whether a drug is socially acceptable or not.

Heroin

Heroin is an **opiate** (a type of depressant drug) and is modified chemically from morphine, which is extracted from opium poppies. Heroin is preferable to morphine as a drug of misuse as it does not stimulate the vomit and nausea centres in the brain. Both heroin and morphine are used as pain-killers for the terminally ill, especially cancer patients.

Psychoactive drugs such as heroin often have their effects by binding, usually with high affinity and specificity, to receptor molecules at synapses. Some drugs block, or antagonise, the action of a neurotransmitter; others imitate or enhance their actions. Heroin has a molecular shape almost identical to a group of neurotransmitters, the **enkephalins**; it mimics their activity by combining with their receptors.

Enkephalins are the neurotransmitters at synapses where sensory neurones from pain receptors connect to relay neurones that convey impulses to the brain (*figure 7.1*). They are widely distributed in the nervous system, including the spinal cord (see *Foundation Biology*, pages 83–86).

Enkephalins are small peptides, just a few amino acids long. In normal circumstances they are released to inhibit the activity of neurones concerned with pain. They are destroyed at the synapse very rapidly, so they do not act for long. Heroin (and other opiates such as morphine) occupy these receptor sites and inhibit the transmission of pain in the same way as enkephalins. Opiates are depressant drugs because they reduce (or depress) the activity of the nervous system, including the respiratory and cardiac centres in the brain. This can prove fatal if activity decreases to such an extent that the diaphragm stops moving or the heart stops beating.

Heroin can be smoked, sniffed or injected into a vein (*figure 7.2*). On the first few occasions when heroin is injected, the user experiences a warm 'rush' and feels contented and very peaceful. This pleasurable state of well-being is known as

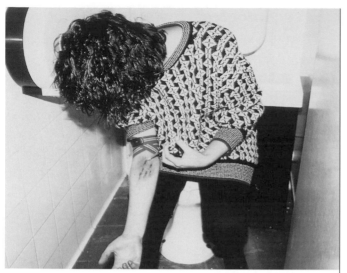

● *Figure 7.2* A heroin addict injecting. When heroin is injected in insanitary conditions using unsterile needles there is a high risk of blood poisoning. If needles are shared with other addicts there is a risk of transmitting blood-borne infections such as HIV and hepatitis B.

euphoria. Users attempt to repeat this euphoric feeling with further doses of heroin.

Effects of heroin on behaviour

Heroin is expensive. As it is illegal it can only be obtained from drug dealers. Some users who may already have felt alienated from society before they took heroin, may become more and more isolated

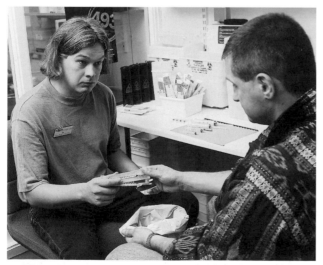

● *Figure 7.3* Charity worker distributing free needles. Needle exchange schemes allow heroin users to obtain sterile needles to avoid the risks associated with sharing needles. They may also receive advice on treatment for their dependency.

from friends and family. Continued use is often associated with difficulty in keeping a job and maintaining normal social relationships. Money to fund the habit may be obtained from criminal activities such as shoplifting, mugging, burglary and prostitution. Heroin addicts tend to neglect their appearance, their health and their families. They often do not eat well or maintain good standards of hygiene. Those who inject heroin put themselves at risk when they share needles. Needle exchange schemes exist to deter addicts from doing this *(figure 7.3)*.

Drug tolerance

People who experiment with drugs as a result of psychological problems probably rely on the drug as a prop. This makes it difficult for them to keep their drug use under control, despite the claims of some that they can control it and do not become dependent upon the drug. If heroin is injected daily for about two weeks, it can cause dependence. There is a progressive decrease in the body's response to the drug. This is known as **tolerance**. The effects of the drug become less intense and so to try to recapture the feeling of euphoria a user may inject larger and larger doses. Tolerance to heroin may occur because more receptors are made at the post-synaptic membranes so that more heroin is needed to stimulate them to have the same effect. When there is no heroin in the body and pain neurones are stimulated, there are insufficient enkephalin molecules to fill the receptor sites and so users feel a keener sense of pain during withdrawal.

The effects of nicotine on the nervous system are described on page 48. Tolerance to nicotine may develop in the same way as to heroin. Nicotine interacts with receptors for the neurotransmitter acetylcholine. These may become more numerous in a smoker, or the sensitivity of the receptors to nicotine may decrease, so the smoker increases the number of cigarettes to maintain the same effect. Smokers who switch to low tar and low nicotine brands often smoke more cigarettes each day to maintain their intake of nicotine.

SAQ 7.2 _____

Describe the effects of heroin on the nervous system.

SAQ 7.3 _____

Suggest some advantages and disadvantages of needle exchange schemes for drug users.

Drug dependence

Dependence occurs when there is a compulsion to take a drug for its mood-altering effects, or to avoid the discomfort, or even agony, of withdrawal. Two aspects of dependence are recognised: **physical** and **psychological dependence**.

Physical dependence

If a drug becomes involved in metabolism, as heroin does when it combines with opiate receptors, the body makes certain adjustments. When the drug is no longer taken, severe physical withdrawal symptoms can result *(table 7.1)*. Together these symptoms comprise the **abstinence syndrome**. The body becomes physically dependent on heroin; it cannot function properly without it.

Smokers become physically dependent on nicotine. When they give up the habit they often experience severe withdrawal symptoms which soon pass if they smoke another cigarette. Smokers often experience anxiety, restlessness, difficulties in concentrating and also a craving for nicotine when they are deprived of the drug. This physical dependence makes it difficult for smokers to give up their habit.

Psychological dependence

There is also an emotional component of dependence. This is a continual craving for the euphoric effects of a drug and is quite separate from any physical dependence. Users enjoy the routine of taking drugs at certain times or in certain circumstances. Alcohol, for example, can become a compulsive pleasure. It is thought that this may occur because alcohol stimulates the production of enkephalins in the brain.

Alcohol

Alcohol (ethanol) is a small molecule and is soluble in both water and fat. It has weak electric charge so it can pass across the lipid bilayer of the cell surface membranes very readily. This explains how alcohol comes to be distributed throughout the body so quickly.

After drinking alcohol, about 20% is absorbed into the blood by the stomach, the rest by the small intestine. Men have an enzyme, alcohol dehydrogenase, in the stomach lining. This lowers the alcohol level a little as it is absorbed. Women either do not have this enzyme, or have smaller quantities. The same quantity of alcohol has a greater effect on women because they tend to be smaller, and also have a smaller quantity of water in their bodies than men of the same size. As a result the blood alcohol concentration (BAC) is higher.

The quantity of alcohol in drinks is measured in units. One unit is 8 grams of alcohol, which is about the quantity metabolised in an hour. One unit is roughly equivalent to half a pint (290 cm^3) of ordinary strength beer, one third of a pint (193 cm^3) of strong beer or cider, one pub measure (24 cm^3) of spirits (such as whisky, brandy, vodka or gin), a small glass (125 cm^3) of wine or a glass (50 cm^3) of sherry.

Once in the blood, alcohol is quickly distributed to all the areas of the body. Little enters

Heroin	Nicotine	Alcohol
stomach cramps	headache	mild tremor of the hands
diarrhoea	stomach pains	nausea
sweating	irritability	sweating
fever	insomnia	weakness
headache	increased appetite	headache
runny nose and eyes	gain in weight	
dilated pupils	craving for a cigarette	
nausea	anxiety	
insomnia	tiredness	
weakness	sweating	

● *Table 7.1* Withdrawal symptoms from heroin, nicotine and alcohol

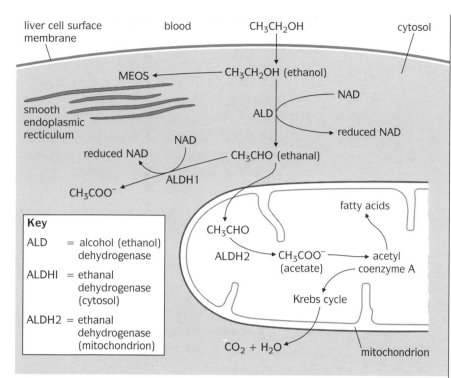

● **Figure 7.4** Metabolism of alcohol in liver cells. Alcohol is metabolised by enzymes in the cytosol and in the mitochondrion. The microsomal ethanol oxidising system (MEOS) is in the smooth endoplasmic reticulum and normally only metabolises 10% of the alcohol oxidised in the liver.

the fat tissue (adipose tissue) under the skin or around the organs such as the heart and kidneys, because fat tissues have a limited blood supply. As alcohol circulates, it enters the liver and is metabolised. It also enters the lungs and kidneys to be excreted. About 2 to 4% of the alcohol consumed is lost in breath and the same proportion in urine. This explains why tests of breath and urine can be used to measure the concentration of alcohol in the blood.

Alcohol is oxidised by liver cells to provide energy and to make 'carbon skeletons' for the synthesis of fatty acids (*figure 7.4*). The first step involves converting alcohol to **ethanal** (also known as acetaldehyde). This occurs in the cytosol. Ethanal is further metabolised in mitochondria where it is oxidised to 'active' acetate, which may either enter the Krebs cycle or be used to synthesise fatty acids.

As alcohol is metabolised, it alters the ratio between the reduced and oxidised forms of the coenzyme nicotinamide adenine

dinucleotide (NAD). As more of the reduced form accumulates, less NAD is available for other metabolic reactions. There is too much to be oxidised in the mitochondria and much of the reduced form is oxidised by conversion of pyruvate into lactate. Some is also used for the production of amino acids and fats with a reduction in the production of glucose from amino acids (gluconeogenesis) and an increase in the concentration of fat in the blood. Mitochondria use reduced NAD generated in alcohol metabolism to generate ATP in preference to fatty acids. As a result fat builds up inside liver cells. The accumulation of fatty droplets in liver cells is most noticeable in binge drinkers who consume large quantities of alcohol at one time. If they abstain from drinking for several days the fat droplets disappear. However, if there is continued drinking of excessive quantities of alcohol, fat remains in the cells and disrupts their proper functioning. The British Government makes recommendations on sensible drinking levels to try to reduce the harm to health from excessive drinking. These were first published in 1987 and updated in 1995 (*table 7.2*).

Date of Government recommendations	Men	Women
1987	21 units a week	14 units a week
December 1995	3–4 units a day	2–3 units a day

● **Table 7.2** UK Government recommendations for sensible drinking

SAQ 7.4

a Explain why recommended alcohol limits for women are lower than those for men.

b Suggest why the UK Government changed its recommendations about sensible drinking to a daily basis rather than a weekly one.

Alcohol tolerance

Habitual drinkers acquire alcohol tolerance as the liver adapts to the presence of alcohol by increasing the production of enzymes that metabolise it. The microsomal ethanol oxidising system (MEOS) plays a minor role in occasional drinkers, but in people who consume large quantities its activity may increase by up to three times. The liver oxidises alcohol at a faster rate resulting in larger quantities being required to maintain the same concentration in the blood and therefore the same mood-altering effect. Nerve cells in the brain also become less responsive to alcohol.

Alcoholic liver disease (ALD)

Ethanal is produced at twice the rate in habitual drinkers than in occasional drinkers. It is potentially very toxic as it is highly reactive. It reacts with proteins to form complexes; interferes with enzyme active sites and structural proteins in cell membranes, mitochondria and the cytoskeleton; and inhibits protein synthesis and other aspects of cellular metabolism. The changed proteins are often recognised as foreign and antibodies are formed against them. This form of auto-immunity probably plays a part in damaging liver tissue, leading to alcoholic liver disease. The high fat and low glucose concentrations in the blood, caused by a reduction in gluconeogenesis, lead to malfunction and disease in the brain, liver and blood vessels. Irreversible damage may be done and can lead to premature death as a direct consequence of alcohol and ethanal.

There are the following stages to ALD.

- *Fatty liver*

  Most of the fat stored in the liver is present as droplets in cells. The liver is swollen with cells full of fat droplets and plasma proteins unable to leave cells because of damage to the intracellular transport mechanisms. There are high plasma concentrations of fats and cholesterol. This affects almost everyone with moderate to high alcohol intake. It is usually reversible if drinking stops. In severe cases it may take four to six weeks.

- *Hepatitis*

  Individual cells are damaged and die. The liver becomes inflamed and damaged cells are replaced with fibrous tissue. There are swollen cells with wispy cytoplasm with much fat stored in them. If this is severe it may give rise to jaundice (the yellowing of eyes and skin that results from the inability of the cells to excrete bile pigments), nausea, loss of appetite and abdominal pain. There is a very high risk of hepatitis developing into the third stage of ALD, cirrhosis. If drinking stops, then the liver returns to normal.

- *Cirrhosis*

  The liver cells are gradually replaced by fibrous tissue rich in collagen fibres *(figure 7.5)*. The liver appears nodular in appearance and hardens. Cells regenerate within lobules, but the cells in these nodules do not receive a good blood supply. Liver functions deteriorate and jaundice gets worse. Blood flow into the liver is obstructed and much of it is diverted to the arteries around the oesophagus causing internal bleeding and vomiting with blood. Cirrhosis is not reversible, but if drinking ceases, the progress of the disease stops.

One third of heavy drinkers never develop severe liver disease, another third only develop fatty liver. Liver cancer develops in about one in five cases of cirrhosis.

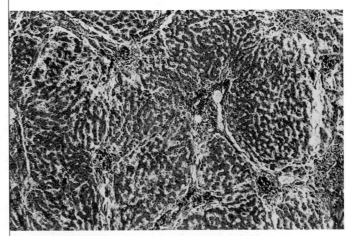

● **Figure 7.5** Photomicrograph of a liver showing cirrhosis. Liver cells have been replaced by fibrous tissue. The collagen fibres disrupt the arrangement of the liver cells.

Alcohol dependence

People who misuse alcohol become physically dependent because they need alcohol to stave off the unpleasant consequences of abstinence *(figure 7.6)*. As alcohol is a depressant, the symptoms of withdrawal are the result of an increased activity of the body systems which were depressed. This is known as **rebound hyperactivity**. In serious cases people who misuse alcohol can suffer from delirium tremens after several days without drinking. There is a persistent tremor, extreme restlessness and agitation, often accompanied by terrifying visual hallucinations. People also become psychologically dependent as the habit becomes engrained in their behaviour and alcohol may afford relief from feelings of anxiety, depression or guilt. People may take to alcohol following a difficult period such as bereavement, loss of their job or divorce.

The features of alcohol dependence are:

- daily consumption of more than 10 units of alcohol;
- increased tolerance;
- BAC of 150 mg 100 cm^{-3} with no signs of drunkenness;
- compulsion to drink and inability to control drinking pattern;
- dominance of alcohol in the person's life.

● **Figure 7.6** A still from the film *The Lost Weekend*, which chronicles the symptoms of alcohol dependence, including hallucinations, blackouts, restlessness and agitation.

Many people who are dependent on alcohol neglect their diet as alcohol provides sufficient energy *(table 2.2)*. But alcohol does not contain any nutrients so there are deficiencies of vitamins and minerals. There are also few antioxidants, and thus no protection against oxidation of lipids by free radicals. This increases the risk of liver damage.

Short-term effects of alcohol on the brain

The effects of alcohol on the brain are associated with the blood alcohol concentration (BAC). After one unit of alcohol is absorbed the BAC in men is about 15 mg 100 cm^{-3} blood and in women 25 mg 100 cm^{-3}. Alcohol depresses brain functions, initially by inhibiting the reticular activating system (RAS), which regulates the front part of the brain, the cerebral cortex. As a result, intellectual facilities are diminished. As the regulation of the cerebral cortex is disrupted, its roles in inhibiting other areas and integrating sensory and motor control are reduced. This leads to loss of coordination, judgement and control over fine movement. With increasing BAC, other centres of the brain are affected, and so too are behaviour and mental abilities. These changes severely affect the ability to walk, cycle or drive. The effects are summarised in *table 7.3*.

Heavy drinkers adapt to alcohol and so perform better than non-drinkers or occasional drinkers at higher BACs. BAC varies from person to person even when they have consumed the same number of units of alcohol. This makes it difficult to predict the BAC to see if it is safe to drive. As a result the best advice is never to drink and drive.

SAQ 7.5
Suggest the factors that can influence the BAC of different people.

Units of alcohol Men	Women	Blood alcohol concentration/ mg 100 cm^{-3}	Effects of alcohol on behaviour	Effects of alcohol on driving
$1\frac{1}{2}$–3	$\frac{1}{2}$–2	20–50	reduced tension, relaxed feeling, increased confidence;	reduced ability to see lights correctly and judge distances; increased tendency to take risks; accident risk is about the same as a non-driver
3–5	2–3	50–80	euphoria, impaired judgement and loss of fine motor control, loss of inhibitions	reactions slower, sensitivity to red lights impaired, shorter concentration span; accident risk is twice that of non-driver
5–8	3–5	80–120	slurred speech, impaired coordination, staggering walk, slowed reaction times	overconfidence, overestimation of driving abilities, reckless driving, impaired peripheral vision, impaired perception of obstacles and ability to assess size; accident risk is four times that of non-driver
8–15	5–10	120–260	loss of control of voluntary activity, loss of balance, erratic behaviour, signs of emotion and aggression	blurred vision; accident risk is ten times that of non-driver
16–26	10–15	260–400	total loss of coordination, difficulty remaining upright, extreme confusion	unable to drive
> 26	> 15	> 400	coma, depression of respiratory centres, death	unable to drive

● **Table 7.3** The effects of increasing drinking and blood alcohol concentration on behaviour and driving ability. The legal limit for driving in the UK is a BAC of 80 mg 100 cm^{-3} blood

Long-term effects of alcohol on the brain

The long-term deterioration of the brain in people who misuse alcohol is mainly due to the shrinkage of brain cells by alcohol-induced dehydration. Alcohol inhibits the release of the hormone ADH, so the kidneys remove more water than they would normally. Cells are also damaged by the shortage of oxygen (hypoxia) and the low blood sugar concentrations which are associated with long-term alcohol misuse. Nerve cells rely, almost exclusively, on blood glucose for their energy. The main loss of cells occurs in the frontal cortex. Capillaries in the brain are often blocked by blood clots.

Alcohol damage to the brain may be acute or chronic. In both cases the symptoms are similar: there is loss of short-term memory and loss of intellectual functions such as calculation, comprehension and learning new tasks. Sleep is often disturbed with a reduction of the important rapid eye movement (REM) sleep and more waking periods in the middle of the night.

Neglect of diet can lead to a deficiency in vitamin B$_1$, which leads to long-term degenerative changes in the brain. The two syndromes involved are:

■ **Korsakoff's psychosis:** loss of memory, inability to learn new material, confusion, dementia;
■ **Wernicke's encephalopathy:** confusion, disturbance of speech and walking, coma.

Effects of alcohol on the peripheral nervous system

Another consequence of vitamin B_1 deficiency is the degeneration of nerves in the peripheral nervous system – the pathways outside the brain and spinal cord. The myelin sheaths surrounding nerves are not maintained and become less efficient. Loss of nerve function causes a loss of sensory awareness in hands and feet and some difficulty in movement. There are feelings of pain, cramps, numbness, tingling and weakness. This is known as **polyneuropathy**.

Social consequences of alcohol misuse

Alcohol misuse is a factor in crime, family disputes, marital breakdown, child neglect and abuse, absenteeism from work, vandalism, physical assault and petty crime. Problems are particularly serious amongst the immediate family of someone who is dependent on alcohol: furtiveness, secrecy and a concern with money come to dominate family relationships. Supplies of alcohol are hidden and securing supplies becomes an over-riding need. Personality traits in people who are dependent on alcohol include:

  jealousy;
  selfishness;
  irritability;
  uncontrolled anger;
  frequent changes of job;
  changes of drinking habit;
  neglect of food intake;
  neglect of personal appearance;
  aggressive behaviour;
  grandiose behaviour.

Families of people who misuse alcohol may suffer as much as, or more than, the individuals themselves. Surveys of wife battering in 1975 found that half of the husbands were 'frequently drunk'. Conflicts between parents are likely to affect children. Between 20 and 30% of cases of intra-family violence or sexual abuse are quoted as being

linked to alcohol. Domestic violence was the most numerous type of assault found by the British Crime Survey in 1995. It is therefore not surprising that every year refuges for women in England have to find places for 25 000 women and children who are seeking to escape from domestic violence. A further 100 000 are given help and support. A worldwide review of domestic violence carried out by an American University in 1990 found that alcohol is a contributory factor to aggressive behaviour. Arguments over alcohol may be the cause of this type of violence, but drunken men can use it as an excuse, maintaining that they are not violent when sober. Neglect is also common as families are abandoned for short or long periods of time. Alcohol is often associated with unemployment, homelessness and psychiatric illness.

It is difficult to measure the social effects of alcohol misuse. Alcohol is implicated in a very wide variety of crimes although much more strongly in some than others. It is impossible to assess with any accuracy the proportion in which alcohol is the causative factor. The best estimates are like those from studies in the 1970s which showed that between 65 to 80% of homicides involved alcohol. Many people in prison serving sentences for burglary maintain that they drink alcohol before committing offences, but that does not mean that offences were committed while 'under the influence'. A high proportion of offenders in prison are heavy or 'problem' drinkers.

Offences in which intoxication is a necessary ingredient are drink-driving offences and being drunk and disorderly. The problem of drunk and disorderly behaviour has become so bad that some councils, such as Glasgow, have banned drinking in public places. Drink is also implicated in cases of grievous bodily harm, sadistic rape and sexual assaults on children.

Drink-driving

In 1979 there were 1650 deaths in the UK as a result of drink-driving offences. In 1993 the number had fallen to 540. In spite of this improvement, nearly ten people die every week in drink-driving accidents and one seventh of these are not drivers. They are passengers, cyclists or pedestrians. This explains why women, who very rarely test positive in breath tests, make up a quarter of the people injured in drink-driving accidents.

A drink-driving incident is defined as one in which one or more drivers or riders either refuse to give a breath test or fail it because they have over 35 μg of alcohol in 100 cm^{-3} of breath. This is equivalent to the legal limit which is a BAC of 80 μg 100 cm^{-3}. The legal limit is an arbitrary value: the effects of alcohol on the nervous system are gradual and do not suddenly become worse at 80 μg 100 cm^{-3}. It was chosen because over this BAC there is a steep rise in the risk of accidents. Legal limits vary throughout the world. In most of Europe it is 50 mg 100 cm^{-3}. There have been calls to lower the limit in the UK or even to make it an offence to drive with any alcohol in the blood.

Statistics on alcohol consumption and some of its social consequences in 1988 and 1993 are given in *table 7.4*.

SAQ 7.6

Comment on the figures given in *table 7.4*.

	1988	1993
Annual alcohol consumption/ dm^{-3} year^{-1} per person over 15 years old	9.7	9.1
Drink-driving offences	105 000	80 832
Drink-driving accidents	14 520	9 480
Drink-driving deaths	790	540
Drunkenness offences	97 552	65 738

● **Table 7.4** Statistics from 1988 and 1993 on alcohol consumption and some of its social consequences

Questions

1 With reference to heroin and alcohol, explain what is meant by the following terms: *drug*, *drug misuse*, *dependence* and *tolerance*.

2 Describe how alcohol is metabolised in the liver. Discuss the long-term effects of excessive alcohol consumption on the nervous system and the liver.

3 Discuss the social consequences of alcohol misuse.

4 Discuss the factors that can lead to people becoming dependent on drugs.

5 Explain the dangers of alcohol misuse in the young.

6 Discuss the steps that governments could take to reduce the number of people who misuse alcohol, and assess their effectiveness.

SUMMARY

In the context of drug misuse, drugs are chemical substances that alter physical or mental functions of the body.

Some drugs are socially acceptable and are readily available or are subject to certain controls. Possession and trafficking in illicit drugs are criminal offences which are punishable by law.

Drug misuse occurs when drugs are taken in hazardous circumstances which are likely to lead to harming the user.

Tolerance is the progressive decrease in response to a drug as the body adapts to its presence. Adaptation may take the form of an increase in receptor sites at synapses or an increased rate of metabolism of the drug. As tolerance develops, an increasing amount of the drug has to be taken to achieve the same effect.

Dependence occurs when a user experiences disturbed physical and/or mental functions when a drug is not taken for some time. Physical dependence develops when a drug is needed for metabolism. Psychological dependence develops when there is a craving or compulsive desire for the pleasurable effects of a drug.

Heroin mimics natural neurotransmitters by occupying receptor sites concerned with the transmission of pain stimuli. Physical dependence develops quickly if heroin is injected. This may alter a person's behaviour quite radically as they become increasingly concerned about obtaining the next dose.

Alcohol is metabolised in the liver to provide energy. Moderate to high blood alcohol concentrations are associated with changes in mood and behaviour.

Fatty liver, hepatitis and cirrhosis are features of alcoholic liver disease.

Long-term degenerative changes in the brain (such as Korsakoff's and Wernicke's syndromes) and in the peri-pheral nervous system are associated with alcohol dependence.

Alcohol is implicated in a range of social problems such as family breakdown, petty crime and drink-driving.

Answers to self-assessment questions

Chapter 1

1.1 Both parents are carriers (Pp):

Parents: $Pp \times Pp$

Gametes: P, p + P, p

	P	p
P	PP	Pp
p	Pp	pp

Child with phenylketonuria is pp.

1.2 The mother is a carrier ($X^F X^f$):

Parents: $X^F X^f \times X^F Y$

Gametes: X^F, X^f, + X^F, Y

	X^F	X^f
X^F	$X^F X^F$	$X^F X^f$
Y	$X^F Y$	$X^f Y$

Boy with fragile X syndrome is $X^f Y$.

1.3 Carcinogens cause mutation of oncogenes in one cell; this cell loses its ability to respond to signals from other cells. The cell divides after mitosis to form a tumour. The tumour is supplied with blood and lymph vessels and the cancerous cells spread to other organs (metastasis).

1.4 These are suggestions. You may disagree with some of these.

Chapter 2

2.1 a

17-year-old males		20-year-old females	
PAL 1.4	11.11	PAL 1.4	7.19
PAL 1.7	13.49	PAL 1.6	8.22
PAL 1.9	15.07	PAL 1.8	9.25

All results in $MJ\,day^{-1}$.

Example of calculation: 17-year-old males at a PAL of 1.4 have a BMR of $(0.074 \times 70) + 2.754 = 7.934$; EAR $7.934 \times 1.4 = 11.11\,MJ\,day^{-1}$.

b Results for a PAL of 1.4 agree with those in *table 2.4* for both the males and the females.

2.2 Males: PAL $1.4 \longrightarrow 1.7 = +21.4\%$;
PAL $1.7 \longrightarrow 1.9 = +11.7\%$

Females: PAL $1.4 \longrightarrow 1.6 = +14.3\%$;
PAL $1.6 \longrightarrow 1.8 = +12.5\%$

Disease	Category of disease								
	physical	infectious	non-infectious	deficiency	inherited	degenerative	mental	social	self-inflicted
scurvy	✓	✗	✓	✓	✗	✓	✗	✓	✗
malaria	✓	✓	✗	✗	✗	✗	✗	✗	✗
measles	✓	✓	✗	✗	✗	✗	✗	✓	✗
cystic fibrosis	✓	✗	✓	✗	✓	✓	✗	✗	✗
lung cancer	✓	✗	✓	✗	✗	✓	✗	✓	✓
sickle cell disease	✓	✗	✓	✗	✓	✓	✗	✗	✗
Parkinson's disease	✓	✗	✓	✗	✗	✓	✓	✗	✗
schizophrenia	✓	✗	✓	✗	?	✗	✓	✗	✗
Creutzfeldt-Jakob disease	✓	✓	✗	✗	?	✓	✓	✗	✗
skin cancer	✓	✗	✓	✗	✗	✓	✗	✓	✓

2.3 An increase in body fat; outcomes associated with becoming overweight or obese (see page 22)

2.4 Requirement for protein increases as body mass increases during growth, then the requirement remains fairly constant when fully grown. Protein is needed for growth of muscles and skeleton and other tissues. Calcium is needed for growth of skeleton: main periods of growth are in infancy and during adolescence. Less calcium is required after growth is complete. Iron is needed for haemoglobin and myoglobin. Females need larger quantities of iron because of menstrual loss. After the menopause their requirement becomes the same as that of males.

2.5 The EAR for males is $11.51 \, \text{MJ day}^{-1}$; energy from fat $= 0.35 \times 11.51 = 4.03 \, \text{MJ day}^{-1}$. Each gram of fat provides 37 kJ, so

$$\frac{4.03 \times 1000}{37} = 108.9 \, \text{g};$$

108.9g of fat provides 35% of the daily energy intake.

The EAR for females is $8.83 \, \text{MJ day}^{-1}$; energy from fat $= 0.35 \times 8.83 = 3.09 \, \text{MJ day}^{-1}$.

$$\frac{3.09 \times 1000}{37} = 83.5 \, \text{g};$$

83.5 g of fat provides 35% of the daily energy intake.

2.6 Fat provides $37 \, \text{kJ g}^{-1}$, which is about twice as much as the same mass of carbohydrate. Reducing fat intake will reduce energy intake significantly.

2.7 Solvent in blood plasma and lymphatic systems; solvent in urine; required in tears, and in saliva and other digestive juices; hydrolysis reactions in digestion (e.g. starch $\longrightarrow$ maltose $\longrightarrow$ glucose); heat loss in sweating; solvent for all biochemical reactions.

2.8 a Pregnancy: $8.1 \, \text{MJ day}^{-1}$ for first 6 months; 8.9 for last 3 months

Lactation: $10 \, \text{MJ day}^{-1}$ for first month; $10.5 \, \text{MJ day}^{-1}$ for 4–6 months (if breast milk is main energy source)

b During pregnancy, mothers may use stores of fat to provide energy for growth of the fetus, and will not need to eat extra energy-containing foods until the last 3 months, when the fetus increases in size. After birth, infants grow rapidly and require a high input of energy from mothers' breast milk.

c

Nutrient	RNI
calcium	$700 \, \text{mg day}^{-1}$
iron	$14.8 \, \text{mg day}^{-1}$
zinc	$7.0 \, \text{mg day}^{-1}$
vitamin A	$700 \, \mu\text{g day}^{-1}$
folic acid	$300 \, \mu\text{g day}^{-1}$
vitamin C	$50 \, \text{mg day}^{-1}$
vitamin D	$10 \, \text{mg day}^{-1}$

d There could be as much as 14 days between conception and the first missed period. There may be an even longer delay before pregnancy is confirmed (see page 85). The nervous system of the fetus begins developing during these first few weeks so it is advisable to supplement the diet with folic acid before pregnancy is confirmed to reduce the chances of spina bifida.

2.9 Iron is required for the synthesis of haemoglobin and myoglobin; a deficiency of haemoglobin limits the supply of oxygen to the tissues, leading to slow physical and mental development.

2.10 Slow growth rate; deficiencies in the proteins listed in table 2.1; a less effective immune system (see page 75) and therefore a greater risk of infections, for example measles

2.11 Bread, soya, beans, nuts, cereals and peas are rich in proteins. (Yeast extract is a good source of B group vitamins and vitamin B_{12}.)

2.12 The nuns' diet was probably deficient in vitamin D. Very little of their skin would have been exposed to sunlight.

2.13 The housebound and the elderly. Children and adults who wear completely enveloping clothing (e.g. Asian girls) are also at risk, as are people whose skin is too dark to absorb enough light to synthesise much vitamin D.

2.14 a $6.72 \, \text{MJ day}^{-1}$

b This compares well with EARs for 4- to 6-year-olds: $7.16 \, \text{MJ day}^{-1}$ (males) and $6.46 \, \text{MJ day}^{-1}$ (females), and is considerably higher than the requirements of 1- to 3-year-olds.

c

Nutrient	350 g Unimix	RNI for children between the ages of 1 and 10 years
protein/g day^{-1}	23.87	14.5–28.3
iron/mg day^{-1}	10.78	6.9–8.7
calcium/mg day^{-1}	323.40	350–550
vitamin A/µg day^{-1}	808.50	400–500

Unimix provides enough protein and iron and almost enough calcium. It provides more than enough vitamin A to protect children from infections and to make up for any deficiency that existed before they needed food aid.

2.15 Women have a larger proportion of body fat than men.

2.16 $1.65 \, \text{m} = 81.7 \, \text{kg}$; $1.73 \, \text{m} = 89.8 \, \text{kg}$; $1.83 \, \text{m} = 100.5 \, \text{kg}$.

Chapter 3

3.1 Mouth/nostril; nasal cavity; pharynx; trachea; bronchus; terminal and respiratory bronchioles; alveolar duct; alveolus; epithelium; connective tissue; endothelium of capillary; plasma; red blood cell.

3.2 Large surface area; thin epithelium, therefore short diffusion distance between air and blood; well supplied with many blood capillaries.

3.3 During exercise the bronchioles are wider to allow more air to reach the alveoli to supply the large quantities of oxygen needed during exercise and to remove carbon dioxide.

3.4 Exercise; smoking; excitement; release of adrenaline; sleep; rest.

3.5 With age, the arteries do not stretch as well and there is an increased resistance to the flow of blood. The heart needs to beat harder to overcome this resistance.

3.6 a $10.66 \, \text{dm}^3 \, \text{min}^{-1}$ at MR = 0.8; $17.25 \, \text{dm}^3 \, \text{min}^{-1}$ at MR = 1.6; $27.20 \, \text{dm}^3 \, \text{min}^{-1}$ at MR = 2.4.

b All of the following increase: heart rate, stroke volume, cardiac output, systolic blood pressure, tidal volume, breathing rate and ventilation rate. Blood is diverted away from skin and gut to the muscles. Bronchioles widen.

3.7 Carbon dioxide and lactate are released by muscle cells and diffuse into the blood.

3.8 Adjustments to the cardiac output and ventilation rate (see SAQ 3.9b) do not happen immediately.

3.9 a Level of aerobic fitness, size, age, gender, smoker/non-smoker.

b Lactate accumulates, fatigue sets in and this will force you to stop.

Chapter 4

4.1 Bronchitis: enlargement of mucus glands in airways; increased secretion of mucus; narrowing/obstruction of airways; inflammation; severe coughing; coughing-up of phlegm. Emphysema: digestion by phagocytes of pathways through alveolar walls; loss of elastin; overextension and bursting of alveoli to form large air spaces; decrease in surface area for gaseous exchange; lack of recoiling of air spaces when breathing out; decrease in volume of air forced out from lungs; shortness of breath.

4.2 Deaths from lung cancer lag behind increase in cigarette smoking by some 20 years or more in both men and women. Women began smoking later than men, so rise in death rate did not begin until later. More men than women smoke, and more men than women die of lung cancer. The male death rate started to decrease in 1975, roughly twenty years after the fall in cigarette consumption. Fall in consumption by women began about 1975, but by 1991 this had yet to be reflected in a decrease in mortality from lung cancer.

4.3 Tar: paralyses or destroys cilia; stimulates oversecretion of mucus; leads to the development of bronchitis and emphysema (see SAQ 4.1). Carcinogens: cause changes in the DNA of cells in the bronchial epithelium, leading to the development of bronchial carcinoma – lung cancer.

4.4 **a** total number of deaths attributable to smoking: men = 55 508; women = 39 975.

   b percentages: men = 17.5%; women = 11.74%; total = 14.5%.

4.5 Coronary arteries supply the heart with oxygen and nutrients (e.g. glucose and fatty acids for energy, and amino acids for growth and repair of heart muscle protein).

4.6 **a** Cardiovascular diseases are degenerative diseases; deaths in this age range are premature deaths.

   b (i) The death rates are much higher in North Karelia than Catalonia for all cardiovascular diseases in both men and women. They are higher in North Karelia than the national figures for Finland, but lower in Catalonia than the national figures for Spain.
   (ii) CHD accounts for over half of all deaths in this category in North Karelia, less than half in Catalonia.
   (iii) Strokes are responsible for the lowest number of deaths, but the death rate is still more than twice as high in North Karelia than in Catalonia.

   c men

4.7 A greater percentage of the population of North Karelia has high blood cholesterol concentration and hypertension compared with the Catalonians. The incidence of obesity (BMI >30) is similar in the two populations (especially among women) and there are more men who smoke in Catalonia. This may mean that high blood cholesterol and hypertension carry a greater risk than smoking or obesity. In both regions there are few women smokers – this may account for the lower incidence of cardiovascular disease among women.

4.8 Carbon monoxide: combines with haemoglobin to form stable compound carboxyhaemoglobin, with the result that less oxygen is transported in the blood.
   Nicotine: raises blood pressure; raises heart rate; makes platelets sticky and therefore increases likelihood of thrombosis; decreases blood supply to the extremities.

4.9 Examples: carry out health promotion campaigns to encourage people to give up smoking/not start in the first place; provide more non-smoking areas in public places; provide more sporting/recreational facilities; encourage schools to provide exercise and fitness programmes; promote healthy eating campaigns; encourage screening to identify people with high blood pressure and diabetes.

Chapter 5

5.1 Faeces from infected person contain *Vibrio cholerae*. These bacteria are transmitted to uninfected people in drinking water, contaminated food (e.g. vegetables irrigated with raw sewage or food prepared by a symptomless carrier), or when washing or bathing in contaminated water.

5.2 $\dfrac{10^{13}}{10^{6}} = 10$ million

5.3 Refugees rarely have access to proper sanitation, clean water, or uncontaminated food.

5.4 The visitor can drink bottled or boiled water; and avoid eating salads and raw vegetables.

5.5 When a female *Anopheles* mosquito bites an infected person she takes up some gametes of the parasite. These develop into infective stages which enter an uninfected person when the same mosquito takes another blood meal.

5.6 The resistance of mosquitoes to insecticides such as DDT and dieldrin; the difficulty of controlling the breeding of mosquitoes because they lay eggs in small bodies of water; the resistance of some strains of *Plasmodium* to anti-malarial drugs such as chloroquine.

5.7 People can avoid being bitten by mosquitoes, sleep under nets impregnated with insecticide, use repellents; and use anti-malarial drugs as prophylactics (but not those to which *Plasmodium* is resistant).

5.8 Many cases of AIDS are not diagnosed or reported.

5.9 HIV is a blood-borne virus; blood donations may not be screened or heat-treated for HIV.

5.10 Condoms can split.

5.11 Practise safe sex (e.g. use condoms); do not use unsterile needles; have one sexual partner; do not donate blood if at risk of HIV infection; do not use prostitutes (male or female).

5.12 It is important to give advice to people who are HIV+ to reduce the chances of them transmitting the virus.

5.13a Highest incidence/prevalence in South-East Asia, sub-Saharan Africa, countries of old Soviet Union, India, China, Mexico, Peru, Bolivia.

5.13b Poor nutrition; HIV infection; poor disease control; large cities with poor housing and homeless people; countries with limited health facilities and large numbers of displaced people (e.g. migrants and refugees).

5.14 Viruses only have a few targets for drug action such as the enzyme reverse transcriptase in HIV (see zidovudine on page 59).

5.15 Human cells do not have cell walls; human enzymes for transcription and translation are not identical to those in bacteria.

5.16 B and E. These have inhibition zones larger than the minimum required to be in the sensitive range. These antibiotics could be used together.

Chapter 6

6.1 a The specific immune system has made antibodies against the measles virus. Antibodies are made very quickly during any subsequent infection and prevent the development of the symptoms associated with catching measles.

b Antigen: any large molecule (e.g. protein) recognised by the body as foreign. Antibody: a protein made by the immune system in response to the presence of an antigen and targeted specifically at it.

6.2 Lymph nodes are in areas which are exposed to infection (e.g. lungs and gut). They are also in the neck, armpits and groin to filter lymph flowing towards the vital organs in the body core.

6.3 The lymphocyte nucleus takes up most of the cell; there is very little cytoplasm. Neutrophils have a lobed nucleus, with a larger amount of cytoplasm. The neutrophil is larger.

6.4 $10\,\mu m$.

6.5 By puberty, T cells have matured and left the thymus gland to colonise secondary lymphoid tissue. The thymus has no further use, so decreases in size.

6.6 a An APC (e.g. a macrophage) ingests a pathogen and breaks up the surface molecules into smaller pieces which it then 'presents' on its surface membrane. These pieces of molecule act as antigens. Certain B and T cells attach to the APC and are activated.

b Only some B and T cells have receptors of the correct specificity.

6.7 Clonal selection: APCs activate only those B and T cells which have receptors specific to the antigen presented. Clonal expansion: activated B and T cells divide after mitosis to form clones.

6.8 Humoral immunity: B cells form plasma cells, which secrete antibodies into blood and lymph. Antibodies act on pathogens independently of the plasma cells that secrete them. Cell mediated immunity: T$_c$ cells and macrophages destroy host cells that are infected with pathogens such as viruses, *Mycobacterium* and *Plasmodium*.

6.9 There would be no specific immune response as T$_h$ cells control clonal expansion by secreting cytokines. Some antibodies may be produced, but only a limited quantity.

6.10 a The secondary response to the chickenpox virus is very fast, producing many antibody molecules; viruses are destroyed before they have time to infect cells. (The virus can, however, remain in nerve cells and become active again later to cause shingles.)

b Although both are viral diseases, they do not share any antigens in common, so the antibodies produced against chickenpox are useless against measles. A first infection of measles will prompt a primary response.

6.11 Immunity to one strain does not provide immunity to all of them as they do not all share the same antigens.

6.12 Active: antigens are introduced into the body by injection or by mouth, and stimulate an immune response by B and T cells. This provides long-term immunity but is not immediate as the immune response takes several weeks to become effective. Passive: antibodies are injected into the body to give immediate protection against a pathogen or toxin. Antibodies are soon removed from circulation and no immune response has occurred, so this is a temporary form of immunity.

6.13 Maternal IgG increases during pregnancy as it crosses the placenta; it decreases after birth as it is removed from the circulation. This is natural passive immunity. The fetus does not produce its own antibodies because it does not have any mature T or B cells and develops in a sterile environment. The infant produces its own antibodies shortly after birth as it begins to encounter infections.

6.14 The infant is protected against diseases which are endemic and which the mother has caught or been vaccinated against. For example, measles is a serious childhood infection; the infant is protected for several months by its mother's antibodies. (Note that the infant will not gain passive immunity to any diseases the mother has not encountered.)

6.15 Antibodies are proteins. If children have protein energy malnutrition (see chapter 2) they may not have the ability to produce many antibodies or develop T and B cell clones.

6.16 Every time the parasite changes its antigens a new primary response will be activated. As soon as there are some antibodies in the blood, the parasite exposes different antigens, so making the antibodies ineffective.

6.17 a *Mycobacterium tuberculosis, M. bovis*

b HIV

6.18

mAb	Blood group			
	AB+	O−	A+	B−
anti-A	agglutination	✗	agglutination	✗
anti-B	agglutination	✗	✗	agglutination
anti-D	agglutination	✗	agglutination	✗

6.19 It is important that the recipient is not given blood with a foreign antigen which will stimulate an immune response. Antibodies produced against red blood cells will cause them to agglutinate, so blocking blood vessels.

6.20 The monoclonal antibodies are specific to the antigens which are only found on the cancer cells, nowhere else.

Chapter 7

7.1 Legislation (e.g. laws governing sale and use of drugs such as the Misuse of Drugs Act in the UK); surveys of people's attitudes to drugs; prevalence of drug taking (e.g. percentage of the population who smoke, drink alcohol or take cannabis); general acceptance or rejection of drug takers (e.g. when it is socially acceptable to drink alcohol, but not acceptable to inject heroin).

7.2 Heroin mimics the action of enkephalin neurotransmitters at synapses concerned with pain. It binds to opiate receptors to inhibit transmission of nerve impulses in the pain pathways. This has a pain-killing (or analgesic) action.

7.3 Advantages: the schemes give points of contact with medical and support services for addicts; provide advice about overcoming dependence; encourage use of sterile needles by addicts to reduce chances of sharing needles and transmitting blood-borne pathogens such as hepatitis B virus and HIV. Disadvantages: the schemes appear to make use of drugs acceptable; they could encourage drug users to congregate in certain places, which local people may find objectionable. Schemes cost money to finance, people could argue that limited funds should not be used for helping drug addicts.

7.4 a Women tend to be smaller than men, so the same alcohol intake gives higher BACs than in men. But even when differences in body mass are taken into account, a given dose of alcohol will produce a BAC 25–30% higher in a woman than in a man. Women have a larger proportion of body fat then men and as this receives a lower blood supply, alcohol concentrations in the blood are higher. Also, it is unlikely that women metabolise alcohol in the stomach lining.

b The recommendations were changed to deter binge drinking or consuming a week's 'allowance' on one occasion. This can cause fatty liver, which is associated with alcoholic liver disease. The revised recommended sensible limit is also higher: there is evidence that the consumption of moderate quantities of alcohol by men over 40 and post-menopausal women lowers risk of CHD.

7.5 Gender, mass, body composition (proportion of fat), quantity of alcohol drunk, speed of drinking, drinking with food or not, regularity of drinking.

7.6 Alcohol consumption has remained constant. Drunkenness offences have decreased, but this might be a result of changes in police practice. The number of offences, accidents and deaths involving drink-driving have decreased; this may be a result of the increase in the number of breathalyser tests and public awareness campaigns, and growing public intolerance of drink-driving.

Index (Numbers in italics refer to figures.)